Ancient Peoples and Places

THE
IBERIANS

Antonio Arribas

90 PHOTOGRAPHS
53 LINE DRAWINGS
8 MAPS
5 TABLES

London
THAMES AND HUDSON

THIS IS VOLUME THIRTY-SIX IN THE SERIES
Ancient Peoples and Places
GENERAL EDITOR: DR. GLYN DANIEL

Ancient Peoples and Places

THE IBERIANS

General Editor

DR. GLYN DANIEL

CONTENTS

	LIST OF ILLUSTRATIONS	8
	ACKNOWLEDGEMENTS	13
	INTRODUCTION	15
	CHRONOLOGICAL TABLES	17
I	IDENTIFYING THE IBERIANS	21
	Early Writers on the Iberians	21
	The Iberian Problem	22
	Archaeology and the Iberian Problem	23
	The Ethnological Synthesis of Bosch Gimpera	24
	Recent Studies on the Iberian Problem	26
II	THE LAND	30
	Physical Features	30
	The Climate	36
	The Vegetation	37
III	FORMATION OF THE IBERIAN PEOPLES	40
	The Basic Iberian Ethno-Cultural Element	42
	Colonists and Natives	47
IV	THE PEOPLE	61
	How They Lived	61
	How They Fought	73
	How They Spoke and Wrote	87
V	HABITATION SITES AND HOUSES	97

VI SOCIAL LIFE, TRADE AND ECONOMY 116
Political and Social Institutions 116
Economic Foundations 119
Industry 124
Crafts and Craftsmen 124
Trade 126
Coins 127

VII RELIGION AND RITUAL 131
Religious Beliefs 131
Life after Death 137

VIII IBERIAN ART 152
Architectural Sculpture 155
Zoomorphic Sculpture 156
Human Sculpture 158
Small-scale Sculpture: Votive Offerings 162

IX POTTERY 165
Andalusian Pottery with Geometric
Decoration 167
Pottery of the Southeast 169
Pottery with Human Scenes from Liria and
the Spanish Levant 170
Pottery from the Ebro Valley 172
Catalonian Pottery 174

X TARTESSIAN-IBERIAN JEWELLERY 179
Tartessian Jewellery 179
Andalusian Jewellery of the Fifth Century
B.C. 186
Jewellery from the Levantine-Catalan Region 188
APPENDIX 190
BIBLIOGRAPHY 194

Contents

SOURCES OF ILLUSTRATIONS   202

THE PLATES   205

NOTES ON THE PLATES   253

INDEX   265

ILLUSTRATIONS

PLATES   1 Gold ear-ring, La Aliseda

2 Gold clasp and part of a belt, La Aliseda

3 Gold bracelet detail, La Aliseda

4 Gold ear-ring, Santiago de la Espada

5 Gold diadem, La Aliseda

6 Jewellery, El Carambolo

7 Gold plaque, El Carambolo

8, 9 The Sphinx of Haches

10 The Beast of Balazote

11 Head of Seated Lady of Verdolay

12, 13 Head of a *kore*

14 Wing of a stone sphinx, Villaricos

15 Damaged cist of polychrome limestone

16 Pyxis, Peal de Becerro

17 Attic krater by the Black Thyrsos painter

18 Native imitation of Attic column krater

19 Decorated pot, Almedinilla

20 Globular vase, Peal de Becerro

21 Statuette of the Goddess of Fertility

22 Dama of El Cerro de los Santos

23 Dama de Elche

24 Architectural fragment, Elche

25 Capital, Cortijo del Ahorcado, Baeza

PLATES 26 Iron bit, Almedinilla
27 The Carriazo Bronze
28 Silver damascened hilt of a falchion
29 The Cazurro Vase
30-33 Walled enclosure of Ullastret
34 Air view of Sanctuary of El Cigarralejo
35 Sandstone horse votive offering
36 Bifacial sandstone relief of a horse
37 Sandstone relief of she-ass and foal
38 Sandstone horse's head, detail
39 Bronze votive Dama offering a dove
40 Small bronze horse, El Palmar
41 Three bronze male votive figures
42 Relief of The Tamer, Villaricos
43 Limestone relief of a woman and a warrior
44 Male and female *consort* offerers
45 Female head with mitre headdress
46 Dama sculpture, El Cerro de los Santos
47 Dama seated on a throne
48 Headless seated male and female figures
49 Male head, El Cerro de los Santos
50 Male head, El Tolmo de Minateda
51 Male head, El Cerro de los Santos
52 Hind and fawn relief, Osuna
53 The 'Lioness' (bull) of Sagunto
54 Limestone bull, Osuna
55 The Osuna flute player
56 Boy rider on horse, Osuna
57 The horn player of Osuna
58 Vase of the Dragons, Hoya de Santa Ana

9

PLATES

59 Silver fibula, Los Almadenes de Pozoblanco
60 Damascened belt clasp, Peal de Becerro
61 Vase of the Warriors, Archena
62 Vase of the Goats, Verdolay
63, 64 Lid and urn, Oliva
65 Warriors, detail of an urn, Oliva
66 Scaling a city's walls, detail of an urn, Oliva
67 Vase of the Winged Goddess, Elche
68 La Pepona de Elche
69 Kalathos vase, Sidamunt
70 Entrance gateway, Tivissa
71 Two silver vases, Tivissa
72 Silver vase, Tivissa
73 Silver patera with wolf's head, Tivissa
74 Silver patera with lion's head, Tivissa
75 Silver-gilt diadem, Mogón
76 Silver plaque from dagger sheath, Mogón
77 Silver belt clasp, Mogón
78 Gold necklace with lion's head
79 The treasure of Jávea
80 Iberian inscription on limestone block
81 Stele with rider and shield, Palermo
82 Iberian silver coins from Catalonia
83 Silver drachmas
84–86 Silver denarii
87–89 Bronze asses
90 Iron firedog, Puig Castellar

FIGURES 1 *Map: The Iberian Peninsula, pp. 32–3*
2 *Distribution of Greek and Phoenician colonies, p.48*

FIGURES 3 *Woman seated on high-backed chair, pottery sherd, p. 63*

4 *Flute-player, pottery sherd, p. 64*

5 *Procession of women holding hands, pottery sherd, p. 64*

6 *Ritual funerary dance, pottery sherd, p. 65*

7 *The 'Acrobat', p. 65*

8 *Painted head of a woman, pottery sherd, p. 66*

9 *Two cloaked figures, pottery sherd, p. 67*

10 *The 'Lady of the Mirror', pottery sherd, p. 70*

11 *Belt buckle, p. 71*

12 *Small plaque, p. 72*

13 *Soldiery and musicians, vase detail, p. 74*

14 *Warrior wearing a cuirass, p. 76*

15 *Battle between two warriors, p. 76*

16 *'Frieze of the Warriors', reconstructed, p. 77*

17 *Warrior with plumed helmet, pottery sherd, p. 78*

18 *Battle scene, pottery sherd, p. 79*

19 *River battle, vase detail, p. 80*

20 *Warrior bearing a* caetra, *p. 80*

21 *Horse with 'parasol' over its forehead, p. 85*

22 *Horseman armed with falchion, vase detail, p. 86*

23 *Distribution map of inscriptions, p. 88*

24 *Comparative table of inscription signs, p. 89*

25 *A Tartessian inscription, p. 90*

26 *Inscribed piece of lead, La Serreta, p. 92*

27 *Signs of the South Iberian alphabet, p. 93*

28 *Signs of the Levantine Iberian alphabet, p. 95*

29 *Distribution in map of Iberian settlements and cemeteries, p. 98*

30 *Plan of Ullastret, p. 102*

31 *Plan of Puig Castellar, pp. 106-7*

The Iberians

FIGURES   32   *Siting of entrance towers, Tivissa, p. 108*

33   *Plan of La Bastida de Mogente, pp. 112–13*

34   *'Pomegranate Harvest', pottery sherd, p .120*

35   *Fishes on pottery from Liria, p. 122*

36   *'Winged Goddess', pottery sherd, p. 132*

37   *Symbolic cult scenes, p. 134*

38   *Distribution map of Iberian sanctuaries, p. 135*

39   *Limestone cist, p. 145*

40   *Galera grave, section and decorated wall, p. 147*

41   *Grave 75, Galera, plan and section, p. 148*

42   *Main tomb, Toya, p. 149*

43   *Reconstructed wagon-wheel, p. 150*

44   *Map of sculpture finds, p. 153*

45   *Limestone stag, p. 157*

46   *The 'Seated lady of Verdolay', p. 159*

47   *'Horn-player' on limestone block, p. 161*

48   *Distribution map of Iberian pottery, p. 166*

49   *Native krater imitating Greek type, p. 168*

50   *Prow of flat-keeled boat, pottery sherd, p. 171*

51   *'Vase of the Birds', p. 172*

52   *Figures on pottery fragment, p. 173*

53   *'Hunter and his dog', vase detail, p. 174*

54   *Stag-hunt, vase detail, p. 175*

55–57   *Fragment of decorated kalathos, pp. 176–7*

58   *Two small cups, p. 178*

59   *Distribution map of jewellery and metalwork, p. 180*

60   *'Braserillo' and bronze flagon, p. 181*

61   *Gold breast-plate, p. 183*

62   *Necklace of pendant seals, p. 185*

63   *Gold pendant with human figure, p. 186*

64   *Gold ear-pendant, p. 186*

Acknowledgements

I WISH TO THANK all those who, by their learning and their encouragement, have helped with this book.

In the first place, Professor J. Maluquer de Motes with whom I was able to discuss the main problems over the years during sessions of the Seminario de Arqueologia of Barcelona University. His knowledge of the Celtic world and his insight concerning Tartessos have provided the foundations upon which my work was built.

Secondly, my wife—Gloria Trias—whose *Catálogo de las cerámicas griegas en España y Portugal* proved invaluable.

My grateful thanks also go to my colleagues and friends who participated in 'I Symposium de Prehistoria Peninsular' (Pamplona, 1959). In particular, to M. Tarradell and D. Fletcher, on the eastern part of the Peninsula; to J. Cuadrado, on the southeast region; to A. Blanco, on Andalusia; to A. Beltrán, on Lower Aragon; to J. Ma. Blázquez, on the primitive religions of the Peninsula.

I also owe much to the tutelage of the eminent archaeologists P. Bosch Gimpera, L. Pericot, M. Almagro, A. Garcia y Bellido, and J. de Mata Carriazo.

I would like to thank Mrs. Celia Topp for so ably translating my Spanish text; Eric Peters for many valuable suggestions and, not least, Dr. Glyn Daniel, General Editor of the 'Ancient Peoples and Places' series for inviting me to contribute to it.

Acknowledgements to the various institutions and individuals who have supplied illustrations (some not previously published) will be found on p. 202. I am specially grateful to Antonio Bregante for some particularly fine drawings, and to Mr. H. A. Shelley of Cambridge for drawing the maps.

A. A.

Introduction

ANCIENT TEXTS enable us to identify a group of peoples who dwelt along the coast between the Rhône and the Pillars of Hercules. They are known as 'Iberians'—the term being used in a geographical and not an ethnical connotation. According to the written sources the interior was inhabited by Celtic barbarian tribes.

Archaeology and its cognate sciences—epigraphy, philology and numismatics—seek to isolate the Iberians in time and space.

In order to understand these peoples and their distribution during the second period of the Iron Age (when they were already in contact with the Greek and Phoenician colonists) we must bear in mind that the land in which they lived varied in relief, climate and ecology. For that reason it seems logical to discuss the land of the Iberians with reference to definite areas—Catalonia, the Ebro valley, the Spanish Levant (the name by which the eastern part of the Iberian peninsula is known), the Southeast, Upper and Lower Andalusia—rather than in general terms. This division also agrees with the variety of ethnical and cultural elements of the Iberian peoples and proves helpful in tracing the effects of settlement phases in the various regions of the Peninsula.

The combination of these different native cultural strains with the distinctive character imposed by colonization gives us no more than a piecemeal picture of the way of life and of the social, political and economic organization of Catalonia, the Spanish Levant, the Southeast and Andalusia. The system of urban community and of government varies with each region. In Andalusia the cities predominate; in the Spanish Levant and Southeast the native centres are influenced by the colonial entrepôts and grouped in their vicinity; the Ebro valley and Catalonia are areas of towns lacking undue colonial influence.

The art of warfare and the typology of weapons show uniformity among all the peoples of the Iberian region. But they are not sufficiently distinctive to allow us to isolate these peoples from others of the Peninsula.

For all these reasons it is impossible to distinguish an Iberian cultural unity though various cultures can be identified among the Mediterranean and southern peoples of Iberia. These localized and individual cultures coincide with the geographical regions and with the native formative elements.

Nor is it possible to distinguish essential traits in the field of religious beliefs and funerary ritual. The rite of incineration is not exclusive to the Iberians since it was also practised by Greeks and Celts. Noticeable differences exist between the religions, beliefs and practices of the peoples of the South (where they are very elaborate and oriental in inspiration) and those of the Spanish Levant and Catalonia.

With regard to art we shall find some basic traces of unity within a vast variety of very local and limited styles. That will oblige us to think in terms of independent schools, illustrating the different native reactions to the contribution of peoples from the Eastern Mediterranean.

Finally, the classical root of Iberian art and the homogeneity of the alphabet and language provide the only criteria which permit us to use the term 'Iberian peoples'. And here it will also prove necessary to distinguish between the Tartessians (Turdetanians) of the South and the Iberians of the rest of the coastal belt of Iberia.

Historical Events	Dates B.C.
Celts in the Peninsula	800
Phoenician domination over Tartessos	
Rhodian foundation of Rhode (? Rosas)	700
Punic foundation of Ibiza (654 B.C.)	
Journey of Colaius of Samos (c. 650). Independence of Tartessos	
Phocaean foundation of Massilia (c. 600)	600
Phocaean foundations of Hemeroskopeion? and Mainake?	
Hegemony of Massilia over Catalonia	
Battle of Alalia (c. 539–538)	
Periplus of Avienus (c. 530 B.C.)	
Romano-Carthaginian treaty of 509	
	500
Iberian mercenaries in Himera (480 B.C.)	
	400
Delimitation between Rome and Carthage (at Cape Palos), (348)	
Iberian mercenaries in the Carthaginian army (342)	
Pytheas forces the blockade of the Straits (c. 330 B.C.)	
Rebirth of the Greek entrepôts of the Southeast	
	300
237. Carthaginian domination up to Cape Nao	
226. Delimitation between Rome and Carthage (at the Ebro)	
221. Hannibal attacks Saguntum	
218. The Romans in the Peninsula	
209. End of Carthaginian control in the Peninsula	
206. Rebellions of Ilergetes and Turdetani	
200. Rebellions of Suessetani and Sedetani	200
196. End of the Turdetanian rebellions	
195. The Romans enter the Meseta	
138. End of the Lusitanian wars	
133. Occupation of the Meseta (Celtiberia). Fall of Numantia	
	100

Archaeological Events

Dates B.C.	S.E. France Catalonia	Ebro Valley	East and S.E.	Andalusia	Meseta and N.W.
800	HALLSTATT C Urnfields: Moulin de Mailhac, Tarrasa, Agullana I	HALLSTATT C (Peninsular types) Phase III of Cortes de Navarra	SURVIVALS OF MEDITERRANEAN BRONZE II	TARTESSOS Phoenician - Cypriot - Rhodian trade (Ria de Huelva c.750)	ATLANTIC BRONZE II
700	Beginning of Grand Bassin I de Mailhac Parrallí (Ampurias)	Phase II of Cortes IRON (Excised Pottery) Cabezo de Monleón Roquizal del Rullo		Rhodian - Corinthian trade (Jerez helmet) c.630 ORIENTALIZING ART Aliseda, Carambolo	Castros of the Meseta (Cogotas I)
600	Agullana II c.575 Oldest Greek imports at Ampurias and Ullastret	End of Phase I of Cortes; San Cristobal de Mazaleón	URNFIELD INFILTRATIONS (Villaricos) ORIENTALIZING ART (Balazote, Haches)	(Cruz del Negro, Acebuchal, Ceal)	Contacts with Tartessos (Sanchorreja, Berrueco)
500	Grand Bassin II, cemetery of the N.E. wall of Ampurias (Attic imports) Beginning of local Ionian imitations PSEUDO-IBERIAN POTTERY	Tossal Redó POST-HALLSTATT CULTURES	IBERIAN POTTERY AND SCULPTURE		POST-HALLSTATT CULTURES

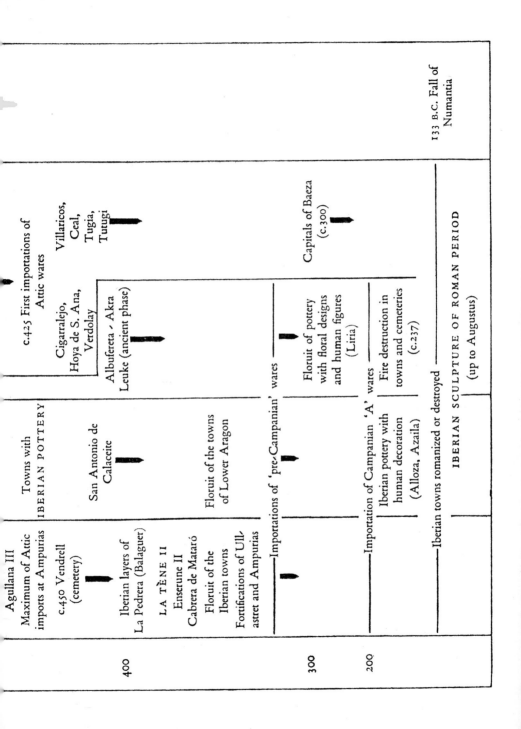

133 B.C. Fall of Numantia

Agullana III
Maximum of Attic imports at Ampurias

c.425 First importations of Attic wares

Villaricos,
Ceal,
Tugia,
Tutugi

Cigarralejo,
Hoya de S. Ana,
Verdolay

Albufereta ⁄ Akra
Leuke (ancient phase)

Capitals of Baeza
(c.300)

Towns with
IBERIAN POTTERY

San Antonio de
Calaceite

Floruit of pottery
with floral designs
and human figures
(Liria)

Floruit of the towns
of Lower Aragon

Importations of 'pre-Campanian' wares

Fire destruction in
towns and cemeteries
(c.237)

c.450 Vendrell
(cemetery)

Iberian layers of
La Pedrera (Balaguer)

LA TÈNE II
Enserune II
Cabrera de Mataró
Floruit of the
Iberian towns
Fortifications of Ull-
astret and Ampurias

Importation of Campanian 'A' wares
Iberian pottery with
human decoration
(Alloza, Azaila)

Iberian towns romanized or destroyed

IBERIAN SCULPTURE OF ROMAN PERIOD
(up to Augustus)

400

300

200

CHAPTER I

Identifying the Iberians

EARLY WRITERS ON THE IBERIANS

AT THE WESTERNMOST LIMITS of the classical Mediterranean world the Greeks sited Hades, the abode of Dis. Along the coast of southern France and the Iberian Peninsula, between the Rhône and the Pillars of Hercules, dwelt a group of peoples who, during the Iron Age, created the cultures we call Iberian.

Greek mariners had made contact with these peoples by the first half of the first millennium, and their stories, compounded of truth and legend, were accepted by the Mediterranean folk.

From the fifth century B.C. it is possible to obtain a clear notion of the ancient authors' concept of the Peninsula and of its peoples and it is then that the names 'Iberians' and 'Iberia' first appear.

Strabo notes that 'according to the ancients' Iberia occupied the zone lying between the Rhône and 'the Isthmus', and Scymnos refers to Iberia as a region where the Phocaeans founded two trading posts: Agde and Rhodanussia.

Avienus includes under the general term 'Iberians' all the peoples of the coast between the river Jucar and the Orano (which must be the Rhône). The author of the Massiliot Sailing Book names certain peoples forming part of the Tartessian confederation—the Cilbiceni, the Massieni, the Gymnetes, the Etmanei and the Ileates.

According to Hecateus, Iberia is the general name applied to western parts although the names 'Iberians' and 'Tartessians' were interchangeable in a wide sense.

Until the time of Polybius, writers called the Peninsula 'Iberia' and the inhabitants of the coast 'Iberians'; in the interior dwelt nameless barbarians. It was easier to make geographical distinctions than ethnic ones (as Strabo later realized) and the historians did not trouble to discriminate between the various tribes of the Peninsula.

Where the Iberians are concerned, ancient writers have concentrated on relations with other peoples mentioned in the texts—the Sicani and the Ligurians. Avienus sites the Sicani beside the river Jucar and they have been related to the people of the same name who, according to Hecateus, Philistos, Ephorus and others, arrived in Sicily after being expelled from their land by the Ligurians. The presence of the Ligurians in the Peninsula (inferred from the same sources) has always been founded on philological grounds unsupported by archaeological evidence. For that reason present opinion favours the theory that the dividing line between Sicani and Ligurians was the Rhône and that neither people ever reached the Peninsula.

THE IBERIAN PROBLEM

Research on the Iberians began with the interest taken by eighteenth-century antiquaries in the origin of the Basque language. It was Alexander von Humboldt who, in 1821, advanced the hypothesis that the Basques were descendants of the Iberians.

During the second half of the nineteenth century, up to 1893 when Hubner published his *Monumenta Linguae Ibericae,* the philological elements of the Iberian problem were derived from geographical studies. Around that time numismatists identified the mints of Iberian coins, assessed their worth and began a serious study of the whole subject.

In 1905 the application of linguistics to toponymy was rendered fashionable by Wachernagel, and Camille Jullian in 1909 studied the *Periplus* of Avienus in this light and defined the problem of the Ligurians in Iberia.

The first attempt at a synthesis was made by Phillipon in 1909. He accepted the ideas of Jullian and d'Arbois de Jubainville with regard to the existence of a pre-Celtic Ligurian group and of a pre-Iberian group in Western Europe.

Leite de Vasconcellos, in the Peninsula, gave substance to a theory which was to have its greatest exponent in Adolph Schulten. This postulated the African origin of the Iberians; at the same time, he affirmed their survival as the Basques.

All this had its roots in the fields of linguistics and of ethnology. But, at the start of the present century, archaeology intervened in the Iberian problem.

ARCHAEOLOGY AND THE IBERIAN PROBLEM

The find of the Dama de Elche in 1897 was so sensational that it gave rise to the excavations of Engel and Pierre Paris at the stronghold of Osuna (Seville). At the same time J. R. Mélida discovered the first sculptural groups in the Cerro de los Santos (Albacete). These events and the excavations of George Bonsor in the region of the Guadalquivir between Mairena and Carmona (province of Seville), together with the unearthing of the cemetery of Almedinilla (prov. of Córdoba) by Maraver and of that of Villaricos (prov. of Almeria) by Louis Siret, enabled Pierre Paris to present the Iberian problem in archaeological terms.

But it fell to Schulten's lot to establish a systematic chronology of the written sources and to present an ethnological synthesis. He postulated a native Ligurian population on which were superimposed the Iberians from Africa and the Celts from Central and Western Europe. All these formed the Celtiberian complex in which the Iberian element predominated.

According to Schulten, the group of cemeteries unearthed on the Meseta by the Marquis de Cerralbo must be attributed to the Celtiberians since these graves were sited in the area supposed to belong to that people. However, as the typology of the finds indicated a date earlier than that assigned to the Celtiberians—namely, the third century B.C.—Schulten was forced to call them Celtic or pre-Iberian. The supposed 'Iberian' character of Numancia, centre of the anti-Roman resistance in the Meseta, did not bear out those facts. The assumption that the Celts were earlier than the Iberians on the Castilian Meseta originated from this false premise.

B. Taracena proved that Schulten's hypothesis was incorrect when he discovered that the Iberian element was very sparse in the pottery of Numancia and attributed its presence to commercial contacts. In addition he found in the 'castros' near Numancia a stratigraphy which could be correlated with that of the same city.

THE ETHNOLOGICAL SYNTHESIS OF BOSCH GIMPERA

Between 1916 and 1936 fieldwork continued under the auspices of the Junta Superior de Excavaciones y Antigüedades. To this period belong the excavations in the sanctuary of Collado de los Jardines (prov. of Jaén) and at other sites in the Llano de la Consolación (prov. of Albacete), as well as at the sanctuaries of La Luz (prov. of Murcia) and of La Serreta de Alcoy (prov. of Alicante). This work in Andalusia and the Southeast culminated in the excavation of two most interesting cemeteries, Tugia (Peal de Becerro, prov. of Jaén) and Tutugi (Galera, prov. of Granada).

At the same time, in the Catalan region, the recently created Institut d'Estudis Catalans (1915) controlled the work of a school directed by Professor Pedro Bosch Gimpera. The fieldwork covered the region between the towns of the Catalan coast and those of Lower Aragon in the interior.

Numerous towns in the Ebro valley were examined and their plans drawn; typological sequences of the finds proving contact between this zone and Numancia were established. Among these towns the most worthy of mention are San Antonio de Calaceite, San Cristobal de Mazaleón, Les Escodines, and Piuro del Barranc Fondo whose various phases now require a fundamental revision.

In 1932 Bosch Gimpera published his *Etnologia de la Peninsula Iberica*. It was a landmark in the study of the primitive peoples of the Peninsula by reason of its author's powers of synthesis, scientific outlook and lucid exposition. This synthesis was soundly based on a combined study of the archaeological material, its background and the typological evolution of the finds in accordance with the ancient texts.

According to Bosch, the historical Iberian peoples resulted from the fusion of two native elements—the 'Capsian' and the 'Pyrenean'. To these must be added a new and predominating one, the Ibero-Saharan which, in some areas, intermingled with the Celtic element. The Iberian culture, *sensu stricto*, would have its origin in the old stock (Bosch's Capsian) in contact with the colonizing peoples, since he did not admit that the Ibero-Saharians ('Hamites', coming from North Africa) possessed sufficient native talent to create Iberian art and culture.

The Iberians proper would occupy all the Spanish Levant and the Ebro valley and spread through Catalonia and the South of France, one wave reaching the north and the centre of the Peninsula. Besides these, Bosch recognized the 'Tartessian' peoples with a very local evolution caused by the stimulus of the native peoples of Andalusia.

Bosch Gimpera's brilliant synthesis was followed in its general outlines by a number of Portuguese, among them Mendes Correa. Professor Manuel Gomez Moreno of Madrid, who in 1925 had crowned a long period of study with his scholarly elaboration of the Iberian alphabet, propounded a very personal thesis which agreed in general with that of Bosch Gimpera.

Bosch Gimpera's synthesis was rendered possible by colla-
boration in the fields of Anthropology and Linguistics. The
anthropologist Aranzadi established in 1915 the original duality of Basques and Iberians and linguists such as Menendez
Pidal (1918), Meyer Lubke and H. Schuchardt (1925) demolished Schulten's supposed parallels between Basques and
Ligurians.

RECENT STUDIES ON THE IBERIAN PROBLEM

An important new period of investigation began in 1939.
Excavation of Iberian towns of the Spanish Levant such as
Liria, Covalta, La Bastida de Mogente and Rochina, discovered between 1920 and 1936, proceeded apace. The stratigraphy of the town of Archena (prov. of Murcia) was investigated; systematic excavation of the sanctuary and cemetery
of El Cigarralejo (Mula, prov. of Murcia) was begun and
work on the cemetery of El Cabecico del Tesoro de Verdolay,
in the same province, was resumed.

In 1941 yet another event of vital importance occurred: the
Dama de Elche and the sculptural group from Osuna were
returned by the Louvre. A study of these, together with excavations in the Spanish Levant and the Southeast, made it possible for Professor A. Garcia y Bellido to postulate a late date—
Roman in the ultimate phases—for Iberian art.

This revolutionary assertion provoked scepticism among
Spanish archaeologists since the late date advanced by him for
Iberian art gave rise to a whole series of apparently insoluble
problems. There were, for instance, texts written in the Iberian
alphabet which could be read but not translated. The exposition of Avienus' *Periplus* could no longer be logically interpreted. Bosch's system of chronological sequences was very
vulnerable owing to its obvious stratigraphical deficiencies.
Finally, Garcia Bellido's strong arguments in favour of a late

date for Iberian art did not solve the problem of its origins. Many of the Andalusian and Southeastern sculptures obviously had close connexions with the Greek world of the Archaic period. Similarly, Iberian painted pottery was related to Sub-Geometric and Geometric patterns. And yet no arguments could be found to give them an early date.

On the other hand the development of Celtic studies inclined Spanish archaeologists to concentrate their attention on that civilization and to ignore the Iberian culture which continued to be the subject of local studies. The gigantic strides in Celtic and Indo-European philology, begun with the work of Pokorny in 1936 and 1938, were another powerful factor in this attitude.

Approaching the problem from a linguistic viewpoint, Pokorny distinguished various Indo-European invasions of the Iberian peninsula. The first was that of the Illyrians, which was followed by two Celtic waves, Goidels and Brythons. Menendez Pidal, in 1939–40, identified Pokorny's Illyrians with some Ambroni or Ambro-Ligurian Celts, already partly Indo-Europeanized. Following him, Martinez Santa Olalla assigned dates to these events, without any documentary evidence, placing the Goidelic invasion in 650 and the Brythonic in 250 B.C. Martin Almagro echoed the work of his predecessors and hastened to revive Bosch Gimpera's classification.

The progress of Indo-European philology in the Peninsula, due to the work of Uhlenbeck and Tovar, finally ended the Basque-Iberian thesis. As a result, the partisans of the Iberians saw themselves in an impasse when endeavouring to explain the Iberian by means of the Basque.

Although certain advances have been made in recent years, no new argument towards solving the Iberian problem has as yet been formulated. But views expressed at the First Symposium of Peninsular Prehistory, held at Pamplona in 1959, indicate that we may be nearing a solution.

Meanwhile, further steps are being taken and lines of investigation pursued. Thus excavations are now carried out with due attention to stratigraphy. The sanctuary and cemetery of El Cigarralejo, and the cemeteries of Verdolay and La Hoya de Santa Ana (the last in prov. of Albacete) provide chronological data for the sculptures and ceramics of the Southeast. At Los Castellones de Ceal (prov. of Jaén) it was established that Celtic burials lay below the Iberian.

The stratigraphy of the settlements must be considered alongside that of the cemeteries. Some trial pits at Ampurias, the excavations at Ullastret (prov. of Gerona) in progress since 1952, the findings recorded at Cayla de Mailhac and Ensérune (France), as well as the publication of work in Spanish Levantine towns (such as La Bastida de Mogente), provide the basic elements for elaborating a chronology of the Iberian world.

Complementary to this is the excavation of the Celtic towns of Cortes de Navarra and Cabezo de Monleón de Caspe (prov. of Saragossa). Although these towns were not occupied by the Iberians, some of them show levels of settlement pertaining to the Iberian culture. This is also clearly visible at La Pedrera de Balaguer (prov. of Lérida) and indicates the lines along which research into the origins of Iberian towns in the Ebro valley should proceed.

Caro Baroja has initiated the careful study of institutions and of political, social and economic organization; J. M. Blazquez has done likewise concerning religion.

Iberian numismatics are in process of being most competently studied by Navascués, P. and A. Beltrán, F. Mateu and J. Gimeno. Philology has wisely been restricted to the elaboration of isogloss maps which will permit the study of similarities and variations in the area of the Iberian alphabet.

The spread of Iberian pottery throughout the Western Mediterranean has also been followed up and its contacts with other cultures suggest chronological parallels. Most interesting in this connexion are the finds in various Phoenician establishments of North Africa and the recognition of new kinds of pottery which indicate the strength of Eastern penetration.

Nor is this all. Recent years have witnessed renewed interest in the problem of Tartessos. The quest initiated by Schulten for the mythical city whose name and fame were known from ancient texts seemed at an end. But today Tartessos is beginning to be considered as the focus of a particular art distinct from Iberian art proper. Such was the line adopted by Professor Garcia Bellido in 1955 when he declared a series of supposedly Phoenician bronze *oenochoi* found in Andalusia to be of native origin. Blanco studied the technique used in the manufacture of certain Andalusian jewellery and reached the same conclusion; this conviction is also shared by Professors Maluquer and Kukahn. Thus the claim for the existence of a city or territory sufficiently rich and powerful to produce such works of art has been established. And such a centre, at the meeting point of Eastern and Celtic stimuli, open to all influences, must surely have been sited in the Tartessian region, the focal point of the finds.

We are still only in the initial stages and may expect more precise results with the adoption of improved techniques and the study of a wider group of objects. The resurrection of Tartessos is a theme dear to the heart of Spanish archaeologists and the attempt to provide archaeological corroboration for the texts presents an exciting topical task.

CHAPTER II

The Land

THE CASTILIAN MESETA forms the centre of the Iberian Peninsula and covers three-quarters of its area. Here the Palaeozoic is overlaid on either side of the eroded range of the Central Massif by Tertiary sediments and only comes to the surface in the peneplain of Estremadura.

The landscape of the Meseta, based on clays and marls, consists of horizontal *páramos* occasionally intersected by residual hills. It is divided from East to West by a series of mountain ranges which separate the valleys of the great rivers, the Douro, Tagus and Guadiana. In its northern region the Meseta reaches a mean height of 600–800 metres in contrast with the lower southern plateau which at no point exceeds 400 metres above sea level.

The topography of the Iberian peninsula differs from province to province. In the south, fertile valleys gaze at rugged, mostly barren and rocky mountains. There is not a great abundance of water. The central plains are dry and alternate extremes of heat in summer with extremes of cold in winter. The northern region nearest the Pyrenees has many forests, most of them evergreen.

After its centuries of cultivation more than 16 per cent (about 16 million acres) of the Iberian peninsula is sterile. Roughly only one third of the land (approximately 40 per cent, about 41 million acres) is cultivated. Approximately 44 per cent of the ground (say 44 million acres) is covered by forests and pastures.

Some 12 million acres are given over to the cultivation of cereals. The remainder of the cultivated acreage yields olives, grapes and fruit as well as those products (such as potatoes and corn) more recently introduced into the Peninsula.

With its harsh climate the Meseta was in antiquity (and still is) a land of cereals and the granary of Spain. Its ancient economy was based on the cultivation of wheat, barley and rye, on the pasturing of sheep and the rearing of pigs.

The backbone of the Peninsula is formed by the Iberian Massif, a series of limestone ranges extending from the Cantabrian Mountains to Cape Nao and bounding the central plateau. This massif is the main watershed of the peninsula separating the great rivers which cross the plain and flow into the Atlantic from the shorter ones flowing into the Mediterranean.

Surrounded by marginal mountains of Alpine origin the upland plateau was predominantly Celtic, in contrast with the regions facing the Mediterranean which were peopled by Iberians. These regions comprise the foothills of the Pyrenees, the Ebro depression, Catalonia, the Valencian coastline, the Southeastern zone and all the southern part of the Peninsula.

Catalonia. The coastal zone between the Pyrenees and the mouth of the Ebro has a rich and varied flora due to the mild climate and the proximity of the sea. The Catalan Mountains, 250 km. in length, separate this coastal region from the interior. This mountain system consists of an inner range, a low-lying hilly zone with wide tracts of cultivated lands, a coastal range and finally a rich plain controlled by Iberian settlements.

A series of such settlements, of very varied nature, can be traced in Catalonia. They were peopled by the Cerretani, the Andosini and the Arenosi of the Pyrenean valleys, the Ausetani of the interior, the Indicetes of the northern coast, the Laietani around Barcelona and the Cossetani to the North of Tarragona.

Fig. 1

The Ebro Valley. The river Ebro runs through the northeastern part of the central plateau to the Mediterranean in a large depression lying between the Iberian Mountains and the Pyrenees. Its upper and middle reaches flow through barren and salty moors and steppe-like lands (Los Monegros) but from the

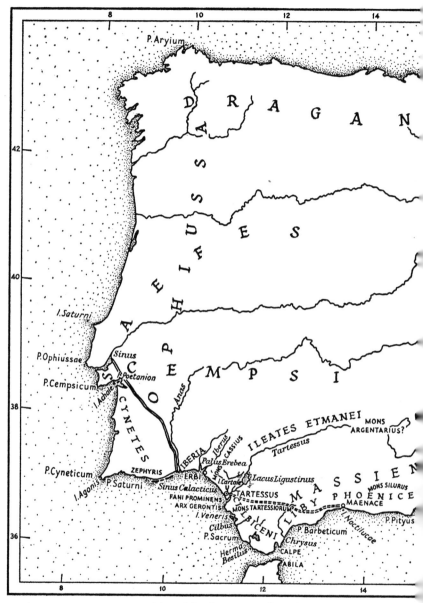

Fig. 1. The Iberian Peninsula according to the Ora Maritima

terpreted by Schulten with modifications by Garcia Bellido)

c

point of confluence with the Segre the landscape changes to the rich plains of Urgel. This was the land of the Ilergetes who were in contact with the Celtiberian peoples (Vasconi in the North and the Belli and Titi to the South). Before reaching the sea the Ebro breaks through the Catalan Mountains in a rugged defile. In its lower reaches it glides through a low-lying region until it eventually forms a vast marshy delta.

The Spanish Levant. South of the mouth of the Ebro the Iberian Mountains stretch to the coast. They form a defensive glaçis in the mountainous and irregular region of the Maestrazgo, reaching to Cape Nao and, in the interior, to the depression of Albacete.

The coast narrows towards the South at Saguntum but the alluvial deposits of the rivers Turia and Jucar widen it again at the alluvial platform of Valencia. The seaward encroachment of the Alicante ranges cuts through this portion of the coastal fringe.

In the regions described dwelt the Iberians proper—the Edetani and the Contestani.

The Southeast. This is the region of the Deitani and the Mastieni of the *vega* of the river Segura (Murcia). The mountains through which the Segura flows are of complicated pattern and form part of Penibaetica. Beyond the steppes of Almeria the corridor of Baza leads into the *vega* of Granada. The eastern slopes of the Sierra Nevada descend abruptly to the sea. The narrow coastal strip of the Mediterranean enjoys a warm climate in its flat zone, due to the winds from the Sahara tempered by the proximity of the Sierra Nevada. Here was the land of the Bastetani.

Andalusia. The south of the Peninsula is Andalusia, watered by the Guadalquivir. Here was the Baetica of the Romans, the Turdetania of the Iberians and the much-disputed region of Tartessos. The plain of the Guadalquivir, between the Sierra Morena in the North and the mountain ranges of Baetica to the South, is a land of fertile fields.

Upper Andalusia. The Sierra Morena which forms the southern edge of the central Meseta and falls abruptly to the depression of the Guadalquivir is an eroded plateau (peneplain) furrowed by many small river courses. Above all a grazing region where summer transhumance is practised, it is more closely related to the low southern Meseta than to the valley of the Guadalquivir. For this reason the Oretani who dwelt in Upper Andalusia in protohistoric times were a connecting link between the cultures of the central plateau and the Turdetanians who inhabited the valley of the Guadalquivir.

The Baetic mountain ranges are actually either isolated massifs or made up of low hills. Between the Baetic Pre-alps and Penibaetica runs a longitudinal narrow depression forming the fertile open *vegas* of Antequera, Granada and Guadix. Westwards, the two mountain systems draw closer to each other and subdivide into calcareous ranges which unite at Ronda. Thence the depression continues southwards to the Straits of Gibraltar.

The Valley of the Guadalquivir. Within this frame of mountains forming the valley of the river Guadalquivir lies a region with marked geographical and cultural features. The plains watered by the river's course constitute a triangle narrowing towards the interior with its base on the Atlantic seaboard. The river rises at a height of 1,300 metres and descends rapidly into a low-lying zone where it meanders through surface Tertiary formations.

This region is the Andalusian plain filled with olive groves where large estates (*latifundia*) still practise the ancestral economic system of cultivation. Mountain profiles are scarce and marginal, being mainly eroded hills such as Los Alcores de Carmona, Montilla and Jerez. The plain is separated from the lower Baetic ranges by a zone of marginal hills which contain the olive groves of Jaén and Córdoba in the North; westward lie the lowlands where cereals and vineyards flourish.

The valley of the Guadalquivir, domain of the Tartessians and the Turdetanians, was coveted by neighbouring peoples.

Thither came the Lusitanians of the West and the Celtiberians of the Meseta in the course of their forays. They remained as settlers, either as mercenaries of the peaceful farmers of the valley or as paid exploiters of the region's mineral wealth.

Such is, in general outline, the physical aspect of those parts of the Peninsula where lived the peoples who created the Iberian civilization, which varies considerably according to the regions. Undoubtedly such differences, arising from varying ethnic and cultural heritages, are far more marked among the peoples of Lower Andalusia—the Tartessians and the Turdetanians—and the Iberians of the east coast than among the inhabitants of the coastal strip in between them.

THE CLIMATE

Because of its configuration, the Iberian Peninsula resembles a small continent. The mountain wall surrounding the upland Meseta determines its continental climate and the area is subject to both continental and Atlantic influences.

Iberia is divided into a dry and a humid zone. In the former —by far the more extensive—precipitation is sparse (the maximum height of the southeastern region is less than 200 metres); the latter comes under oceanic influences. Wind and rainfall are determined by differences in temperature between the interior, where summer and winter bring extremes of heat and cold, and the peripheral regions.

The harshness of the Meseta climate was noted by the Roman soldiers. Thus, in the winter of 153–152 B.C., Nobilior, obliged to winter outside Numancia at an altitude of 1,200 metres, had to watch his soldiers die of cold and exposure. Aulus Gelius noted that the strength of the North wind was such that 'it fills the mouth when one speaks and blows over an armed man and even a loaded cart'. This same wind caused floods of the river Ebro and uprooted the native houses.

The Mediterranean Coastline. The Spanish poet Martial speaks of the soft climate of the Mediterranean coasts in contrast to the harshness of the Meseta winters. In general, all the Mediterranean coastal regions enjoy a mild climate which, by reason of the river system, reaches well into the interior. Climatic oscillations are more marked here than in the Atlantic zone; precipitation is infrequent but sometimes violent. The mean temperature of January is the mildest for the whole of the Peninsula.

It is possible to distinguish various climatic sectors along the Mediterranean coast. Dryness becomes more marked as one progresses towards the steppe-like Southeast. The climate of the southern zone of the Sierra Nevada is tempered by the proximity of this wall of permanent snows.

The Depressions of the Ebro and Guadalquivir. In these two regions the climate is again different, being determined by their peripheral position, their general low level and the fact that they are enclosed by mountains. In both, the climate is warmer than that of the Meseta and their temperature variations greater; precipitation is scarce and the summers are extremely dry.

But in the valley of the Guadalquivir (which is nearer to the Atlantic) these general conditions tend to be less pronounced. The South Atlantic cyclones bring warm wet winds in winter; these, impinging on the mountains of Sub-Baetica, condense and water the plains. Conversely, the valley of the Ebro at the same season is subjected to peninsular anticyclones and, in consequence, has only a low rainfall.

THE VEGETATION

The geography and climate of the Iberian Peninsula have combined to produce a vast variety of vegetation. Contrasting with the landscape of woods and meadows of the humid zone the Mediterranean flora penetrates deeply into the interior where both zones meet. Three-quarters of the Peninsula has a Mediterranean flora, and certain species such as the evergreen oak (Q. *ilex*) grow everywhere. Conversely, some species of Atlantic flora—for instance the beech (*Fagus*)—extend south of the Central Massif.

The oak (Q. *robur*) is proper to the Atlantic climate and forms extensive woods in the lower zones of the Pyrenean slopes.

Catalonia and the Spanish Levant. The humid Mediterranean regions—the Catalan cordilleras and the Pyrenean foothills—produce *Quercus faginea* with all its varieties, and chestnut; they undoubtedly represent the optimum zone of the evergreen oak (Q. *ilex*) which predominates over some species of the pine. In antiquity this zone of Mediterranean climate extended from Catalonia to Valencia and also included the valley of the Guadalquivir and the mountains of Baetica and the Sierra Morena, all of which regions are nowadays very denuded.

The Southeast and Andalusia. Along the coast from Valencia to the Sierra Nevada the semi-arid Mediterranean climate produces steppe-like types of flora. In this region (and in general in the South of the Peninsula) heat, drought and the destruction of the rocks, due to extremes between day and night temperatures, have caused the disappearance of thick undergrowth and reduced it to a minimum of low-level Mediterranean vegetation. This is exemplified by Q. *coccifera* and, in zones of temperate winters, by *Chamaerops humilis* (alligator-pear). Deciduous trees appear in regions where the land rises to a certain height and, on poor soils, evergreen oaks, oleasters and cork-oaks grow. In the Sierra Nevada the altitude favours a type of thick and prickly scrub composed of *Erinacea anthylies*.

The disappearance of woods in the Peninsula is one of the most salient events of its history. Strabo mentions the woods around Numancia and Appian asserts that the Vaccean town of Pallantia was taken after its walls had been breached by great tree-trunks used as battering-rams. If the Meseta plain was covered with oaks, evergreen oaks and junipers, the peripheral mountains and many of their valleys must also have had similar woods. In fact this supposition has been corroborated by classical texts. Pliny tells of an olive wood on the coast of Cadiz which was only a miserable remainder 'of the large and ancient woods of apple-trees which yielded golden fruit'. Another famous wood was sited at the source of the Guadalquivir, close to Tugia, and all the region of Bastetania had its mountains clothed in dense groves.

Chapter III

Formation of the Iberian Peoples

DURING THE NEOLITHIC PERIOD there occurs for the first time a cultural homogeneity in the Iberian peninsula (at least in the coastal Mediterranean regions). The horizon of 'impressed ware' extends throughout this zone and forms a part of the cultural pattern in the western Mediterranean world. Foreign contributions during the Early Bronze Age came from the Near East and an Aegean-Anatolian source, either by sea or via the Danube. The main colonies of the Eastern Mediterranean peoples who brought the megalithic culture to the Peninsula at the beginning of the metal ages were on the southeast coast and on the Guadalquivir and Tagus estuaries. Possibly a secondary megalithic focus in the Central Mediterranean islands led to the Pyrenean megalithic culture.

Metallurgical techniques and certain features of funerary ritual as well as religious beliefs changed during the El Argar period of the Bronze Age. Collective burial in ossuaries gave way to individual inhumation. It has always been assumed that the newcomers travelled to the southeastern shores of the Peninsula by sea. But the cultural and ritual changes only affected a small area, outside of which they appear to weaken and to blend with the old Neolithic tradition.

The native element dating from the El Argar period is the one to be studied because from it stem the peoples of the Levant whom we name Iberians *sensu stricto*. The Celtic invasions through the passes of the Pyrenees which began in the ninth to eighth centuries B.C. altered the ethnic and cultural aspect of two-thirds of the land. The Hallstatt C culture was adopted mainly in the Meseta and the Northwest, to a lesser extent in Catalonia and the Ebro valley, and sparsely in the South and East of the Peninsula.

The introduction of ironworking in the sixth century B.C. radically changed the life of the Iberian peoples. Its spread among the inhabitants of the Peninsula is one of the enigmas of proto-history. The use of iron for weapons and tools begins in phase C of the Hallstatt culture but the clearest and oldest peninsular evidence comes from the Celtic settlement of Cortes de Navarra, in the Ebro valley, in its phase IIb (650–550). In the Spanish Levant, however, no sites of such an early date show any evidence of an iron industry and even in the Catalonian Urnfield cemeteries like Agullana (prov. of Gerona) in its final phase II and in phase III (550–500) iron is scarce. It was only after that date, at a time when commercial contacts with Greeks and Phoenicians might already have made it available, that the native settlements used iron on a large scale.

Technical improvement of weapons altered the entire social and political organization. Pictorial art, as shown by the pottery, bronze and stone statues, jewellery and metalwork of these regions, reflects a somewhat individual outlook on life. But no change was greater than that which took place in religious beliefs and ritual: cremation became universal. This event, so contrary to the old native traditions, implies considerable pressure despite the fact that penetration by Mediterranean colonists must have been weak and only intended to secure a market. On the other hand, even though a Celtic element existed in various areas of the Iberian world, there is no clear evidence of the Celtic rite influencing the Iberian.

Not until we are able to assess correctly the rival influences of both those civilizations and their effects on the Iberian peoples shall we arrive at the truth. At present it is only possible to recognize their active presence and the receptive attitude adopted by the native peoples towards them.

The ethnic and cultural element on which the Iberian cultures are founded is as diverse as are the corresponding geographical divisions of the land.

THE BASIC IBERIAN ETHNO-CULTURAL ELEMENT

For the purposes of this book we have divided Iberia into the following areas: Catalonia, the Ebro valley, the Spanish Levant and the Southeast, and Andalusia.

Catalonia. The native element in this region is represented by the cultural horizon of impressed neolithic ware.

This includes all the 'pit-burials' and cave-settlements, none of which can provide stratigraphical or chronological data. The Pyrenean megalithic culture was superimposed upon this uniform foundation, and its spread at the beginning of the second millennium only covered Upper Catalonia, i.e. the Pyrenees and their foothills.

There thus exists a duality of ritual which suggests an ethnic distinction, and it is also true that the difference in the nature of the land between Upper and Lower Catalonia would have given rise to two distinct economies. The most interesting aspect of this basic Catalan element is its analogy with that of southeastern France, which would explain the similar reactions of the two regions towards the classical world.

This Pyrenean culture (which adopted Beakers at an early stage) slowly evolved under North Italian influence. This is shown at the beginning by pots with knobbed handles and, later, by the distribution of pottery with excised decoration belonging to the Apennine Bronze Age and extending as far as the cave of Seriña (prov. of Lerida). Something of both these traits reaches even further south to the cave of Josefina (prov. of Tarragona) and to Sena (Aragon), region of the pit-burials.

The Urnfield invasions of Catalonia began in the ninth and eighth centuries B.C. The cemetery of Tarrasa (prov. of Barcelona) with Hallstatt C objects (800–700) belongs to an early stage, and although these types are distributed throughout Lower Catalonia their route can be traced in Upper Catalonia. The evidence does not prove a large ethnic contribution but the rite of cremation was certainly introduced. Layers with a concentration of channelled ware at certain caves (Can Montmany de Palleja, prov. of Barcelona) and at settlements such as La Pedrera de Balaguer (prov. of Lérida) indicate the strength of the invasion. This invasion established an agricultural economy in the lowlands, and its peoples endured, on an ever-dwindling scale, until the fifth century B.C.

Around 750 B.C. another Urnfield wave entered Catalonia. It was more powerful than the first and included elements belonging to phases C–D of the Hallstatt culture related to those of southwest Switzerland and northeast Italy. The most typical cemetery is that of Agullana (prov. of Gerona) whose phase III lasts up to 500 B.C. A local variant of this culture known as the Post-Hallstatt extends throughout Catalonia. From the fifth to fourth centuries onwards, the local wheel-turned pottery was superimposed on this cultural foundation.

The Ebro Valley. In the Ebro valley we find a culture which lasted from the Neolithic up to the period of the Atlantic Bronze Age.

Impressed ware has recently been found there, but pit graves and megalithic tombs are lacking. A series of finds proves that the final phase of the Bronze Age persisted throughout the whole of the Iron Age up to the Iberian period. This is shown by axes of Atlantic Bronze Age types from the settlement of Vilallonc de Calaceite (Teruel) and the axe moulds, arrowheads, rods, etc., found at Cabezo de Monleón de Caspe (Saragossa). The earliest Hallstatt period finds are localized in the region of the Central Ebro and indicate a primary Celtic penetration via the Western Pyrenees. The arrival of invasion waves from the Central Pyrenees and the valley of the Segre is marked by a trail of bronze hoards (Organyá, San Aleix, Abella) in the province of Lerida at a later period.

The urnfields of the epoch Hallstatt C–D illustrate a characteristic culture using urns placed in cists under a tumulus;

43

the type site is Cabezo de Monleón de Caspe. Here the fusion of early types of the Hallstatt A and B periods with native techniques produces the excised wares which later spread over the Meseta during Hallstatt C–D.

The frequent occurrence in the Ebro valley of wheel-turned wares above those of Hallstatt C–D and alterations in settlements and houses belonging to this earlier period indicate the end of Celtic culture in this area about the fifth–fourth century B.C.

The Spanish Levant and the Southeast. These geographical regions had a neolithic cultural background, as evidenced by the coastal distribution of impressed ware like that of Cueva de la Sarsa and Cova d'Or (prov. of Valencia). Relations between the Almerian inhumations and the individual pit graves of the Catalan region, via the Southeast and the Spanish Levant, are now being reconsidered because the connecting link is still unknown. During the Bronze I period the culture of Los Millares influenced all the Levantine area of the Peninsula. But, although related cultural elements exist, the megalithic funerary ritual was replaced by collective cave burials. It must also be pointed out that only in the Spanish Levant are echoes of the cultural elements of El Argar (Hispanic Bronze II) found. Between 1500 and the first half of the first millennium B.C. this zone went on reproducing objects typical of the Mediterranean Bronze period. This resulted in the strange and monotonous complex of survivals and archaisms that occur in the foundation levels of all the Iberian towns of these regions.

It is true that in some sites of the Spanish Levant and the Southeast urnfields are encountered but they always appear as intrusions belonging to the sixth to fourth centuries B.C. This poses one of the most interesting problems of this area, since the Levantine urnfields seem to bear no relation to those of Catalonia. The possibility of their having originated in the Meseta and arrived by an unknown route is under consideration.

Thus, in this geographical region, as in no other, the native element was able to develop autonomously the Iberian culture which here appears most clearly and free from foreign influences.

Andalusia. Although the southern region is by far the richest in every aspect, it nevertheless presents enormous lacunae as regards the study of the origins and development of the Iberian peoples.

In caves in Andalusia we find a neolithic facies of impressed and incised pottery upon which is superimposed the megalithic culture.

During the first half of the first millennium a long gap occurs between the final stages of that culture and the initial phases of the Iberian one. There are three centres with relevant material: the regions of the Upper and of the Lower Guadalquivir and that around Villaricos (prov. of Almeria).

Some of the richest cemeteries belonging to the Iberian complex have been excavated in the Upper Guadalquivir but they appear there within an already developed setting and include Greek objects of the fifth and fourth centuries B.C. Such are the cemeteries of Tugia, Tutugi and Basti and various others. Very recently, the excavation of the cemetery of Los Castellones de Ceal (Jaén) revealed Celtic graves of the sixth century B.C. below Iberian tumuli which are dated to the fifth and fourth centuries. The typological relations between the urns of Ceal and those of Villaricos are extremely interesting and imply a higher dating for part of the latter cemetery than was formerly thought possible. A whole series of sites around Villaricos in Eastern Andalusia which flourished from the start of the Metal Ages up to the time of the Iberian spread must now be similarly dated. The only intrusive elements in these sites are the urnfields noted at Parazuelos, Alparatas, Barranco Hondo and Caldero de Qurenima.

In the region of the Lower Guadalquivir are the graves of Setefilla (prov. of Seville) and those excavated between

Carmona and Mairena in the same province. At Acebuchal, Bencarron, Alcantarilla, Cañada de Ruiz Sanchez and other sites Bonsor identified the cremation graves with those of the natives and the inhumation ones with those of the Carthaginians but without establishing positive criteria for such a rigid differentiation. In fact the ivory plaques and combs whose decoration is of a strikingly eastern character were found alike in both types of tomb. A silver fibula and a hooked belt buckle—which have parallels at Le Cayla (Aude) in its phase II (550–475) and at other sites of the Hérault, the Aude and Catalonia (e.g. at Agullana, Camallera)—came from the inhumation tumulus G at Acebuchal.

One of the most interesting sites explored by Bonsor is La Cruz del Negro. Here were found 30 cremation burials aligned in pits and urns of oriental type, perhaps copied locally. The grave goods, consisting of fragments of ostrich eggs, ivory plaques, combs, glass beads, scarabs, etc., suggest a very eastern background. Together with these occurred hand-made clay urns and metal objects proper to the Hallstatt period which have parallels at Le Cayla II, Agullana II and Molá (prov. of Tarragona).

A similarly dual background characterizes the cemetery of Setefilla. Typologically the graves derive from the Hallstatt C–D period and the ornament of the hand-made pottery links up with the cultural horizon of the excised pots of the Meseta (Cogotas) and of the Ebro valley (Redal). The origin of these Andalusian tumuli cannot be traced in the Peninsula; but they bear a likeness to the Celtic ones of the Ebro valley.

This unusual coexistence of Celtic and Eastern elements in the lower reaches of the Guadalquivir accords with Avienus' account of the penetration of Celtic groups to Tartessos and Gades in the sixth century B.C. The Andalusian tumuli would then be those of Celtic chieftains, deeply imbued with oriental customs, who ruled the Tartessian region.

Interest in the Tartessian question has been stimulated by new finds between 1959 and 1961—the treasure of the Carambolo (Seville) and the excavation of Carmona. Considered in conjunction with the recently found jewellery, they present various problems. The attribution of the 'Boquique' pottery to the similar Celtic wares of the Meseta, the acknowledgement of a late date for the burnished ware formerly considered as of Early and Middle Bronze Age type, the appearance of Iberian painted ware in the fifth century B.C. must be re-examined in the light of these discoveries.

The Tartessian world of the first half of the first millennium B.C. is thus seen to have been a complex one: a blend of Celtic and Eastern elements resulting in a still somewhat obscure fusion which is beginning to be considered as a possible origin of the Iberian culture in the fifth century B.C.

COLONISTS AND NATIVES

Written sources place the foundation of Gades (Cadiz) by peoples from Tyre at the time of the Trojan War or a little later. Velleius Paterculus makes the event contemporary with the return of the Heraclids which, according to Eratosthenes, took place towards the end of the twelfth century prior to the foundation of Utica (1178) and Carthage (814). *Fig. 2*

Such an early date for Phoenician trade in the Central and Western Mediterranean is contradicted by the archaeological evidence, according to which Phoenician trade with the West reached its peak in the eighth century B.C. The surrender of Tyre to the Assyrian king Tiglath-Pileser in the year 750 B.C. must temporarily have retarded its activity.

But, despite the lack of facts to uphold tradition, it is hard to envisage the three previous centuries without Phoenician commercial activities. It is supposed that these were based, in the period between 1100 and the eighth century, on direct contacts

Fig. 2. Distribution of Greek and Phoenician colonies

without the establishment of colonies. Indeed, the types of Phoenician settlement tend to support this assumption since they mostly depended on the barter of materials which have perished.

But in order to understand the problem in all its magnitude it is necessary to consider the main motives for trade with the western world—the need for metal.

TARTESSOS OR THE PHANTOM ELDORADO

The name of Tarshish is mentioned in the Bible as that of a prodigiously rich region visited by Phoenician ships.

Today, everything points to Tarshish having been situated in the extreme West, and it may be identified with Tartessos in the Guadalquivir region whose king Geryon was in touch with the Phoenicians from the start of the eighth century B.C. The Tartessians were very soon compelled to fight the Phoenicians, to whom they then remained subject. The period during which

Shalmaneser V and Sargon I (724–720) occupied Phoenicia might well have brought that freedom referred to by Isaiah when he spoke the words: 'Thou, people of Tarshish, no longer oppressed by bonds.' With the restoration of Phoenician power around 680–670 Tarshish again became a subject city.

The kings of Tartessos and their relations with the Phoenicians must have been known by hearsay to the Greeks, perhaps those of Sicily, and Heracles (confused with Melkart) was made to symbolize Geryon in the struggle of the Tartessians against the Phoenicians. The genealogy of the Tartessian kings is based on mythological personifications from king Gargoris in the ninth century to Arganthonios whose reign marks the end of the dynasty. Arganthonios, the long-lived and philhellene Tartessian king, is historically real and is referred to in the story of the journey of Colaius of Samos in the mid-seventh century B.C.

The power of Tartessos was founded on metal. From a remote period the tin trade had been the reason for relations between the South of the Peninsula and the North Atlantic regions. In the period called the Atlantic Bronze Age (1100–800 B.C.) there is evidence of a maritime trade supported by finds of axes and weapons along the Atlantic coasts.

The Pseudo-Scymnos describes Tartessos as a city 'in the Celtic region, famous for alluvial tin, gold, and copper', and Pliny assures us that the tin which ancient peoples believed to be a product of the Atlantic West came from Lusitania and Galicia. The other tin-producing regions, Cornwall and Brittany, must have been exhausted by the third century B.C. but the Phoenicians had already discovered and used them in coastal trade during an earlier epoch.

The *Periplus* of Avienus states that the islands of the Oestrymnides were rich in tin and lead and that the Tartessians were wont to trade with them 'as also the Carthaginian colonists and the peoples who dwelt close to the Pillars of Hercules'.

From this text it seems likely that the Tartessians were the first to use the Atlantic tin trade route, and that, at a later period, they were replaced by the colonists of Gades, mostly of Carthaginian origin, who succeeded in conquering Tartessos.

It is not known whether Tartessos exploited the peninsular tin resources, but certainly the copper mines of the Rio Tinto (prov. of Huelva) as well as the tin trade were the source of its prosperity.

The bronze weapons found when the Huelva estuary was dredged date from the apogee of Tartessian metallurgy. The objects formed part of a cargo en route for Tartessos or some other Mediterranean port and were destined for recasting. The sword types prove their Atlantic origin but the axes are similar to those of Sardinian hoards and the fibulae derive from Syrian and Cypriot prototypes. The date of the fibulae places the Huelva hoard around 750 B.C. but the nature of the objects due to be recast suggests that the wreck occurred when they were already out of date. Could the cargo have come from the North, following the coast? It has been suggested that the ship was descending the Guadiana along a non-maritime route marked out by the sword finds of the rivers Esla and Alconetar. But was Huelva the final port of call? The fibulae of Cypriot-Syrian origin are very like others from the Meseta which must be of much the same period.

A strong current of Eastern trade through Tartessos around 750 B.C. may be inferred. This trade, together with the vicinity of Gades and the archaeological background of El Acebuchal, Carmona, Setefilla and Carambolo, shows that the Tartessian area was imbued with oriental ideas. Phoenicians, Syrians and Cypriots, amongst others, created in Andalusia a cultural background comparable with that established by the Greeks in Magna Graecia.

The independence of Tartessos is manifest in its politics and economy, since the city treated directly with the Greeks, and further evidence is provided by its culture and the creation of a special alphabet for its own particular use.

Perhaps the disaster of Alalia (539–538) was responsible for the fall of philhellene Tartessos and the end of the first Greek entrepôts in the South of the Peninsula. There were some later risings of the Tartessians after 500 B.C., which obliged the Phoenicians of Gades to seek the aid of the Carthaginians. But thenceforth the life of Tartessos was at an end and the Carthaginians again took over the metal trade of the Atlantic.

The Western Mediterranean was in turmoil around 500 B.C. and it is necessary to turn once more to the journey of Colaius in order to understand the rise of other rivals of the Phoenicians in the metal trade—the Greeks.

More is known about the first contacts of the Greeks with Iberia than is recorded of those of the Phoenicians, although chronology is somewhat confused regarding both events.
GREEK
PIONEERS IN
THE WEST

A certain period has been ascribed to the legendary Trojan cycle and the return of the 'nostoi' to their native land and their adventures in the West; these legends, however, were not elaborated until the Hellenistic epoch. A series of Cycladic finds and some objects of the Geometric Period said to be from Marseilles and the nearby Hyères Islands have been related to these fictional travels, but both their authenticity and their provenance are doubtful.

Discoveries, explorations and attempts to establish markets by the inhabitants of Rhodes and Chalcis during the eighth and seventh centuries are known. The Pseudo-Scymnos provides the basis for these travels but its interpretation is fraught with difficulties. Its source must have been Ephorus and it tallies with archaeological evidence. Rhodian objects of around 650 B.C. have in fact been found in the Rhône estuary. The diffusion of bronze *oenochoai* of the period 650–625 B.C. throughout the Mediterranean must be attributed to the Rhodians who founded Gela in 688, after the colonization of Naxos.

The earliest Greek finds of the Peninsula, such as the Corinthian helmet from the river Guadalete (Jerez) or those from Huelva, are datable to about 630 B.C. when there were contacts between Arganthonios and Colaius. Thus there is evidence not only of the Samian's journey but also of the possible existence of the entrepôt of Hemeroskopeion, of the sanctuary of Cape Artemision, of Mainake (Malaga) and of Heracleia (Carteia) towards the end of the seventh century B.C. or the early part of the sixth.

The route of these Peninsular foundations can be traced by the ancient names ending in *oussa,* such as the Pythioussas (the Balearics), of Aegean provenance, perhaps related to the metal trade and certainly prior to the Phocaean colonization.

A long period elapsed between the travels of the *naukleroi,* half traders and half pirates, such as Colaius, and the establishment of entrepôts known to us through archaeology.

COMMERCE AND COLONIZATION IN THE SIXTH CENTURY B.C.

The Phoenician cities of Gades and Ibiza have yielded no objects dating from before the sixth century B.C. At the close of that century it is surmised that other sister establishments such as Malaca (Malaga), Sexi (Almuñecar), Abdera (Adra) and Villaricos (called 'Libyophoenician' in the *Periplus* of Avienus) were founded along the southern coasts.

The reasons for speaking of an earlier trade have already been given and they support the texts which ascribe older foundation dates than those provided by archaeological finds.

The same applies to the Greek establishments of the Southeast (Hemeroskopeion and Mainake).

We know more about the colonies of the sixth century after the foundation of Massilia because the texts agree with the archaeological evidence. Emporion (Ampurias) and Rhode (Rosas), both sited along the Catalan coast in the province of Gerona, resulted from the extension of the Phocaean centre of Massilia—although it is possible that Rhode was founded by Rhodians in the seventh century B.C.

From the Pseudo-Scylax onwards the texts refer to Emporion as a Massiliot foundation and Strabo mentions a first foundation (Palaiápolis) followed by a settlement on the mainland. Archaeology proves that the new city of Emporion was founded about 580 B.C. Other trading posts appeared in the Peninsula: *Pyrene*, near Cape Creus, *Cypsela, Kallipolis,* near Tarragona, *Hyops*, close to the Ebro delta, *Lebedontia*, to the north of Cape Nao. None of these has been located, although recent excavations at Ullastret (Gerona) indicate that this city might possibly be Cypsela.

It is generally accepted that the defeat of the Greeks at Alalia by the Carthaginians and the Etruscans ended Phocaean power. It also marked the end of the southern Peninsular Greek entrepôts and the transference of trade in the Straits to the Carthaginians. We know today that the disaster affected the Phocaean pirates of Alalia, that Massilia's Greek trade was not impaired and that the alliance between Etruscans and Carthaginians proved ephemeral. Nevertheless, it is certain that the Straits remained under Carthaginian domination at the close of the sixth century or the beginning of the fifth, and Pindar affirms that 'one cannot go further than Gades; beyond lies darkness'. Herodotus confirms this misapprehension by his inability to site the Cassiterides owing to the vigilance of the Carthaginians in the Straits.

The rebirth of the Greek western colonial world during the course of the fourth century B.C. gave fresh impetus to old entrepôts such as Alonai (Benidorm) and Akra Leuke (Alicante). It is even possible that this took place as early as around the end of the fifth century. THE ENTREPÔTS UP TO THE ROMAN CONQUEST

That the southern part of the Peninsula then received a strong Greek colonial impact is proved by imports of Attic and southern Italian pottery. Greek commercial power in the South ended shortly before the First Punic war (264–261) and the southern part of the Peninsula was entirely dominated by Carthage. But, as a consequence of that war, the Carthaginians lost their sway over the Massiliots and the Iberians. In 237 Hamilcar landed in the Peninsula and Carthaginian possessions were re-established by his advance to Cape Nao and the destruction of Hemeroskopeion. He built a military fortress at Akra Leuke, and Carthago-Nova became the centre of Punic power.

A series of small treasure hoards like those of Cheste, Mogón and Montgó are datable to this period when Greek trade was curtailed by the Carthaginian advance.

There followed the peace treaty of the year 226 between Carthage and Rome, which established separate spheres of influence south and north of Cape Nao. Neither power adhered to the terms of the pact, and Rome's alliance with Saguntum provoked Hannibal's attack which started the Second Punic War. He invaded the area north of the Ebro between 218 and 201 B.C. on his way to Italy.

The destruction of the greater part of the Greek colonies caused by this struggle and the Romanization of the remainder ended trade relations between Greece and Iberia.

RELATIONS BETWEEN COLONISTS AND NATIVES

In order to understand the nature of the colonial settlements in the Peninsula and the influence they exercised on the natives, one must bear in mind the fact that the only excavated site of that kind is Emporion. The identification of Cypsela (possibly with Ullastret suggested above) would raise the number of known colonial establishments to two.

Up to the present, all attempts to site the other coastal settlements have failed. We may regard Akra Leuke (Alicante) as having been located but its earliest phase does not pre-date the fourth century.

The colonies of Italy and Sicily were villages having an agricultural economy. The importance of the colonies depended on their size and on the fertility of the soil, hence their need for expansion. This was achieved at the expense of the natives who proved easy to subdue because of their inferior numbers and the superior culture of the Greeks. Cultivation of the fields promptly increased as well as commerce and industry, and local production was soon initiated in order to provide trade with the natives.

In southern Sicily a series of settlements which were cultural centres were established on top of prehistoric ones. They were closely connected with the coast and, in turn, became the source of changes which spread into the interior. They were not primitive prehistoric villages but true Greek centres, the product of mixed peoples and of Greek and local influences.

The settlements of the Gulf of Lyons possessed a very distinctive character. Massilia, with its port surrounded by bare mountains, had a poor hinterland. The introduction of vine and olive cultivation could hardly have provided the vast economic resources of the city. Provençal finds of the Archaic Period are sparse and evidence the lack of interest in cultivation and territorial expansion of the Massiliots. On the other hand a series of establishments with a radius of 10–15 km. inland shows the interest of Massilia in securing command of the Rhône-Saône tin trade route.

In antiquity tin was produced in two western localities: Cornwall in England and the mouth of the Loire in France. From Cornwall the metal reached the mainland by way of the Channel and the Lower Seine. Then the tin from both Cornwall and the mouth of the Loire was shipped through Vix and upper Burgundy to the Rhône-Saône valley, the main route to Marseilles and the Mediterranean.

Massilia's concern with the Languedoc was but slight and limited to seeking markets for her local wines. Thus there existed official colonies on the one hand and, on the other, Greek settlements in Provence, not far from the cultivated plains of Narbonne, intended for trade with the natives.

This is the type of commercial relations that must be taken into consideration when studying contacts between Greeks and natives in Iberia. The best parallel for Emporion and Ullastret is provided by Massilia.

Catalonia. The 'Neapolis' of Emporion was a simple trading-post whose initial relations with the natives were far from cordial. It was not a colony with a large population, nor did it possess agricultural economic autonomy. Its hinterland, the plain of the Ampurdan, produced wine and cereals but purely local trade cannot account for Emporion's wealth. These vast resources are attested by imports from the end of the sixth century and also by intensive direct traffic in imported Athenian pottery during the course of the fifth century; at that time this trade surpassed even that of Massilia.

Not a single Greek settlement is known in the interior to indicate any territorial expansion of Emporion. The native towns of the Indicetes within a radius of 50 km. have only a very low percentage of Greek wares at the end of the fifth century. The same applies to the coastal towns around Barcelona, already far removed from the sphere of Emporion's influence.

Ullastret, founded as an Iberian *oppidum* among marshes, like Ensérune in the South of France, has a hinterland similar to that of Emporion.

In brief, the economic effect of such entrepôts on the neighbouring natives must have been very slight. Nevertheless there is bound to have been daily trade and direct contact with the Indicete population settled outside the walls of Emporion. As at Massilia, one must assume that vines and olive trees were planted and that at least the direct relations existing between both peoples were used by the natives to their advantage and resulted in material progress.

The natives owed as little to the Catalan trading-posts in the way of art as they did in other respects. This region has no native art which can compare with that of the South and the Southeast. There is a total lack of such indigenous sculpture as resulted from contact with Greek objects imported into Emporion. One can only speak of an influence on the pottery in so far as the wheel was used by the Indicetes because of contact with the colonists. And there is also imitation of pottery shapes and of the simple decorative patterns on waves from Ionia and Phocaea. Specialized workshops of native potters did not exist in Catalonia until the third and second century B.C. Written sources of Roman times also attest the colonists' influence on textile art and the specialization in linen materials of some native centres. All other evidence of influence on material culture is denied to us, owing to the poverty of the Catalan settlements and cemeteries.

The answer to the riddle of Emporion's wealth is given by its coin types and their widespread distribution in the Peninsula. When Emporion became economically independent of Massilia in the first half of the fifth century B.C. it began to mint its own currency in fractions of the Massiliot drachma, in the same manner as Rhode. From about the year 330 it issued an autonomous type of drachma bearing the legend 'Emporion' written in Greek. On the obverse appears the head of Arethusa, copied from Syracusan coins; on the reverse is a quiescent horse crowned by a flying Victory of Carthaginian type. It is thought that these coins were struck at Emporion in silver coming from Cartagena and Andalusia, in order to recruit mercenaries for the Carthaginians in their Sicilian campaigns.

This would imply that Emporion was friendly to Carthage, an assumption that is borne out by the fact that Hannibal avoided the city on his way to Italy in order to maintain friendly relations with a centre so vital to his army.

Emporion thrived on its maritime commerce with the Carthaginians who provided its metal, and that would explain its lack of incentive in extending its hinterland. There is nothing strange about such a friendship. Carthage traded with Attica at this period; Athens and Carthage had a common rival:

Syracuse. This economic interest which Carthage and Athens had in common was partly due to Emporion, directly in contact with Peninsular events and by its very nature a foreign warehouse of Athens.

The Spanish Levant, the Ebro Valley and the Southeast. Finds of Greek pottery from the end of the fifth century and from the fourth generally occur in Iberia all along the coast. The radius of trade never penetrated deeper into the interior than 50 km. at most. The number of Greek pottery fragments in native settlements along the Spanish Levantine coast and in the valley of the Lower Ebro is extremely limited. Furthermore, they were regarded as luxury objects by the Iberians, who occasionally mended them—thus showing the value that was attached to these pots. Iberian graffiti on these objects also prove that they were cherished as well as prized.

The scarcity of Greek pottery indicates that the Greek coastal settlements were trading-posts for barter and did not seek territorial expansion by the establishment of habitation centres. Relations founded on such a basis must have been both easy and friendly. At Villaricos the native cemetery whose very varied grave-goods include Greek and Punic imports is known, but not so the Greek entrepôt.

A group of Iberian settlements and cemeteries of the fifth–fourth centuries B.C., with strong Hellenic influences, marks an inland Greek trade route to Tartessos via the southeast. And it is this area in particular which most strongly reflects the impact of Greek penetration from a cultural, economic and artistic aspect. This route must be considered in relation to the metalliferous sites of Andalusia. On it lie the Sierra Morena mines, and its coastal starting points are Hemeroskopeion and Villaricos. Another route begins at Akra Leuke and runs through Albacete, Balazote and Villacarrillo to Linares (Jaén). Yet another links Elche with Redovan, Orihuela, Murcia and Cartagena and to this must also be added the one linking

Murcia, Archena, Caravaca, Galera and Baza to Guadix. Finally, from Villaricos via Huercal-Overa, one reaches Baza in the inner hub of trade routes with the Sierra Morena.

This is the area that has produced the greatest number of finds of Iberian sculptures showing marked Hellenic influence. Through it, at an earlier period, the Carmona ivories and the objects from Aliseda (Estremadura) must have travelled if they came by a land route.

The natives of this region soon learned to imitate the shapes and decoration of the imported pottery—both those of Greek and Phoenician-Punic origin. The banded pottery of Carmona, Galera and other sites must be considered as an Eastern product of the Phoenician-Cypriot circuit. It was promptly copied in Iberia and its shapes have nothing in common with those of Carthage and North Africa.

As opposed to this, the variety of shapes and decoration of the pottery from the southeast of the Peninsula is far more akin to the Greek wares which it imitates.

The Phoenician and Punic entrepôts must have been of a similar nature to the Greek. Their position was even more favourable, owing to the proximity of the important mining and commercial area under their control. Toll and traffic levies, the monopoly of the Andalusian trade with its rich fisheries and salting industries, point to a high living standard from the economic point of view.

The problems presented by the impact of Greek and Phoenician ideas on the formation of Iberian art will later be discussed in detail. We know but little of the manner of life and of the husbandry at the entrepôts because of their exclusively commercial nature. The Greeks introduced the cultivation of the vine and the olive, and the Phoenicians greatly influenced the weaving of rich and polychrome materials. The effect of Classical religious beliefs on Iberian civilization compares with that in Magna Graecia and Sicily. The southern peoples of the

Peninsula built sanctuaries in which they worshipped divinities of Eastern Mediterranean pattern and inspiration.

In brief, the study of the native ethnic cultural substratum of the Iberian world and the contributions of Phoenician and Greek colonists who fashioned a mode of life among the Iberian peoples enables us, from the fifth and fourth centuries B.C. onwards, to designate them by the particular name of 'Iberians'.

CHAPTER IV

The People

HOW THEY LIVED

IN ORDER TO DETERMINE the mode of life and the appearance of the Iberians we must resort to sculptural and pictorial records and to descriptions in the Classical texts. These are the only reliable sources, since the custom of cremation has removed all possibility of reconstructing the Iberians' physical appearance from their skeletal remains. But it must be remembered that sculpture may be idealized and pictures schematized, also that written references concerning one set of people cannot be generalized and applied to others; nor is the description of one individual valid for all the rest.

GENERAL QUALITIES

We may assume, from their portrayals in Iberian art, that the people were in all respects similar to those at present living in the same areas. They were a slender race, hardy, wiry and with fine features; to Roman eyes they seemed strange and savage.

We are in an even better position to judge their qualities and defects than their physical appearance. Martial contrasted the civilized Greek with the virile Spaniard of austere aspect, with his abundant and untidy hair and harsh voice—Iberian phonetics were ill-adapted to Roman pronunciation.

Contacts with the colonists and the easy way of life common to the Iberians of the Levant and of the South must have reduced their roughness and rendered them more amenable to civilization. Livy, referring to the peoples of the coast, assures us that they were of a restless nature and avid for adventure; he describes the Lacetani of Catalonia as 'deviam et silvestrem gentem'. Polybius contrasts the Iberians and Africans inured to hardship with the Gaulish Celts of little endurance.

The uneven distribution of fertile lands partly accounts for differences of character and mode of life. The Turdetanians, in contact with the Greek and Phoenician entrepôts, never presented a serious problem to the Romans, whereas the Cantabri of the North were the last Peninsular peoples to be pacified by them.

The recurrent slogan of conquerors in the Peninsula has always been 'Peace and Land'. It was with these words that the Roman, Galba, enticed the Lusitanians into an ambush in the year 150 B.C.; they expressed the sole request made to the Roman Senate by the Hispanic envoys. When Sempronius Gracchus redistributed the land among the natives, the basic trouble ceased but discontent was endemic and required radical reforms.

As a consequence, banditry began to spread. Inherent Iberian rebelliousness, tribal individualism and rough customs must be taken into account when considering this economic and social problem. The Romans took greater trouble to subdue the bandits of the Sierra Morena than the peasants of Contestania or the landowners of Turdetania.

Instances of heroic acts constantly recur in the annals of the Roman conquest of Hispania, and give proof of the esteem in which the Romans held native valour. The Ascoli bronze records the gallantry of a handful of Spaniards fighting far from their homeland.

Native nobility of mind was as notable as courage; the Hispanic peoples responded well to their enemies' generosity. The gentle policy of Hannibal and of Romans like Scipio, Tiberius Gracchus and Sertorius paid greater dividends than their military victories. Scipio's good treatment and flattery of the Ilergete petty kings, Indibil and Mandonius, were rewarded by their friendship. Sertorius enlisted the Iberians, 'eradicating their angry and rebellious aspect and converting their forces of large bandit bands into an organized army.' Nobility of spirit sometimes led to exhibitionism among the Iberians which was both used and abused by the Romans.

*Fig. 3. Decorated vase frag-
ment from Liria depicting a
woman seated on a high-backed
chair*

Martial tells us that the men of the villages left home at dawn WAY OF LIFE
for work in the fields, only returning at dusk. The poet meanwhile dreamed of Rome as he watched the faggots blaze in the
well-stocked and recently replenished hearth.

Village folk hardly used the toga and, when it was used, it
was made to last for many years. The house, of one or more
rooms, had the hearth for its centre: the fire's warmth alone pro- Plate 90
vided comfort. Rectangular or square in shape, raised on a
stone foundation, with walls of adobe or dry stone work,
roofed with branches, the houses were, in fact, huts. We know
little of the furniture; the presence of masonry benches in the
tombs suggests that they may also have been used in the houses.
In a picture forming part of a vase-painting at Liria and in an- *Fig. 3*
other from Alloza we see a figure seated on a chair, but the
great canopied thrones of the Damas del Cerro de los Santos
and of Verdolay must have belonged to divinities or priestesses.

Vaulted niches and shelves within the walls may have served
as cupboards; boards and branches covered with pallets were
no doubt used for rest after work or battle.

Carts, ploughs, yokes for pairs of oxen or mules, farm and
carpentry tools such as sickles, scythes, adzes, cattle shears,
rakes, axes, picks, saws, knives, nails and hammers illustrate
the economy and manner of life of such villages.

Fig. 4. Flute-player from the scene shown in Fig. 5

Plate 55

Fig. 5

Fig. 6

Even more than they portray scenes of daily life, pictorial records show us the love these people had for the chase and for battle. Vase paintings depict men enjoying various sports and hunting with snares and ambushes. Riders hurling javelins at wild boars, casting lines and hooks for fish in the lakes, hunting stags either by harrying them into nets or by throwing *bolas*—all this suggests a tremendous zest for life.

The same trait appears to an even greater degree in religious and festive scenes where music and dancing are depicted. Players of flutes, of the *aulos* (or double flute) and of the *tuba*, frequently occur in scenes on the vase-paintings at Liria, and the lovely *auletris* of Osuna is of an extreme delicacy.

Processions danced towards the sanctuaries to the strains of music, holding hands, forming circles or weaving in and out in accordance with an ancestral Mediterranean tradition. Because of its spontaneity the *danza bastetana* of Liria resembles a popular dance rather than a sacred one, whereas the two warriors facing each other to the strains of flutes and tuba seem more likely to be performing a magico-religious propitiation act or ceremonial funeral games.

We know from Livy that the Iberians went into battle leaping in time with a monorhythmic music and singing martial songs. Hannibal made his army file past a pyre at a ceremony

Fig. 5. Procession of women holding hands (fragment of a decorated kalathos *from Liria)*

during which the Iberians danced with arm and body movements. This type of dance was frequently performed by the
Hispani and it was in this manner that the Lusitanians hon-
oured their chief, Viriatus, at his funerary ceremonies. The same
people went into battle singing hymns like the Greek *paian* and
moving their limbs lightly and rhythmically.

Fig. 6. Ritual funerary dance (on fragment from Liria)

The stone relief found at Osuna, depicting an acrobat, is an
impressive record which provides a parallel with the female
castanet-players and the Cadiz dancers of Roman times.

Fig. 7

*Fig. 7. The 'Acrobat' (limestone block from Osuna).
Height 80 cm., width 40 cm., thickness 11 cm.
Nat. Arch. Mus., Madrid*

It seems that the most backward Peninsular peoples knew the epic poems: Sallust tells us that mothers used to recite tales of ancestral exploits to their sons. For that reason it does not seem strange that the Turdetanians (whose traditions reached back into a remote past) knew their ancestry in verse and rhymed their laws while also recording their heroic deeds in writing.

CLOTHING

Fig. 8

Although neither textiles nor leather from the Iberian period have been preserved, it seems certain that native weaving was influenced by both Greeks and Phoenicians. The Iberian woman's love of clothes and rich adornment are well known to us as is also the fame of certain cities for the fine quality of their materials. Polybius notes the difference between Hannibal's Iberian mercenaries wearing purple-dyed linen tunics and the Celts clad in sheepskins and black woollen stuffs.

Fig. 8. Head of woman (painted on small vase from Liria)

The mantle (*sagulus*) of the Meseta region, made of wool and evil-smelling, contrasts with the Turdetanian ones of purple hue which figure in lists of valuable presents to Rome. It was worn like a poncho, secured behind by a waist-belt. At Osuna a man is shown wearing a cloak open in front with buttoned collar and lapels—the first Spanish cape.

From the year 205 B.C. mantles feature among the tributes paid by the Iberians of Catalonia to the Romans.

Fig. 9. Two cloaked figures (fragment of small vase from Liria)

The main garment worn by men was the tunic. This was short, tight-fitting and sleeved; but the long full robe with pleats was also in use. These garments must have been of linen for the nobility and of wool for everyone else. In some instances warriors wore a tunic which appears rigid, as if made of leather or esparto.

Fig. 9

Breeches are depicted at Liria; they are close-fitting and held up by wide braces which cross in front. A frieze on the 'Cazurro vase' shows two boys dressed merely in a short round skirt chasing stags—a rare instance of undress in Iberian art.

Plate 29

Shoes for everyday work must have been sandals of esparto or leather, like the prehistoric ones found at Albuñol in the province of Granada. Riders and warriors at Liria, however, wear high, loose leather boots with wide tops. The Romanized warriors in the Osuna frieze have full-pointed sandals tied round the ankles by many-twisted thongs.

Iberian women had a way of dressing and possessed a type of beauty familiar to us through the paintings and sculptures. Ephorus refers to an exhibition of garments woven by the women, with awards for the best-cut patterns; it was considered a deep disgrace to fail to obtain a prize in this dress show.

Few things are more complicated than the garments of the offerers of votive gifts and of the priestesses both of the Cerro de

Plates 22, 23
los Santos and of the Dama de Elche. The ceremonial clothes comprised four articles: a shift reaching down to the feet, a dress (either loose or close-fitting), a mantle worn over the shoulders and a veil sometimes attached to it.

The inner garment, of linen, is visible on the Dama de Elche and looks like a chiton secured at the neck by a ring-fibula. A lady of Osuna has one which flows down over her feet. Over this garment the Dama de Elche wears another, pleated slantwise from one shoulder to the opposite under-arm. The Lady of Osuna has wide trimmed sleeves reaching to the wrists and her skirt is vertically pleated.

The long tunic robe, usually belted, is seen on the flute-player from Osuna and on female figurines used as votive offerings. The embroideries and appliqué-work of this garment are equalled only by those of the mantles.

Of all the various garments the mantle is by far the most ornate. It was worn over the shoulders, hiding the arms but leaving the breast exposed. The Osuna offerer wears it crossed over her knees. The figurines are shown wearing one of two kinds of mantle: the first is short, like a knee-length shawl, the second is long, folded from one armpit to the opposite shoulder, falling over the coiled plaits and fastened from beneath. In the same figures the veil (*mantilla*) is draped from the head orna-ment and falls in fringes, framing the face or gathered behind the hair-coils.

Sandals of leather or of esparto, like those of an Osuna offerer, were the common footwear among women.

PERSONAL
ADORNMENT
Both the Turdetanians and the Iberians shared the love of the 'baroque' prevalent among the peoples of the South and East of the Peninsula. A taste for adornment, for being different, and a penchant for noise and colour still persist in those regions.

The male figurines from the sanctuaries have shaven heads with a fringe over the forehead. In some cases this may repre-sent a leather cap which allowed the hair to show in front or to fall in long locks or plaits behind. The stone figures from the Cerro de los Santos have been given short curly hair with side locks and a frontal fringe. The head-dress is merely a band (*tenia*) which gathers the hair over the forehead. Some figures from Liria seem to have pronounced beards, but this custom may have been of a purely local and temporary character.

The women's hair-styles and head-dresses are extraordinary. Artemidorus refers to the Iberian women who 'wear a *tympanion* (kettle-drum) curved against the nape of the neck and gripping the head as far as the lobes of the ears'. He adds: 'Some women fix a small rod on to a pedestal and fold their hair around it, enveloping the whole in a black veil.'

Votive figurines are shown wearing caps forming turbans, conical tiaras, diadems of large loops, plaited fillets and other variations. Beneath the head-dress the hair falls in plaits sometimes carried over the forehead, forming an egg-patterned (*ovolo*) fringe with waves disposed either side of a central parting.

The flute-player from Osuna wears a plait above a cap and a fringe flows down to her forehead from the crown of her head. Two plaits woven into a diadem frame the whole and a ringlet curls backwards above her temples to join the twin tresses. Lively parallels to the votive offerings are found in the paintings of Liria: the graceful 'Lady with a Fan' (or mirror) whose head is crowned with a comb, is a replica of the Dama de Elche or the Dama del Cerro, as are also the 'Hooded Ladies'.

Plate 55

Fig. 10

The Dama de Elche wears a tall comb which must have been mounted on a framework and covered by a *mantilla* bound with a diadem from which hang three rows of pearls. This diadem, like those from Aliseda and Javea, consisted of threads of silver or gold. The so-called Cánovas Head wears a triple row of pearls and, above these, are scrolls and rosettes the distant origin of which is evidenced by the Punic ladies of Ibiza.

Plate 23

The drum-shaped disk which holds in place the plaits of the Dama de Elche would have been of metal with granulated

Fig. 10. The 'Lady of the Mirror' or 'Lady of the Fan' (fragment of a painted scene on a vase from Liria)

decoration; her likeness to *korai* of the fifth century B.C. is quite extraordinary. A similar but less opulent type is also seen at La Serreta. The Gran Dama del Cerro hides the disk under her plaits and on her forehead wears a fillet from beneath which peeps a curled fringe.

In general, earrings are extremely ornate. Some are large and round, others double and discoidal and yet others are long and shaped like a tear-drop. Those from Aliseda and Santiago de la Espada are of true filigree work.

From the simple types of bracelets and armlets of the votive figurines to the intricate examples from Molino de Marrubial (prov. of Córdoba) there is a wide range and variety of patterns.

The Iberians, like the Celts, wore torques which were usually simple rolled wires, as well as pectorals consisting of rings hanging from small chains.

Plate 22

Plate 4

The collars worn by the female figurines are very varied. Some are made of different-coloured strings with circular pendants, others are tippets and still others are thick and misshapen with egg-patterned (*ovolo*) pendants. The Dama de Elche wears three rows of collars. From the uppermost, of spherical ribbed beads of polychrome vitrified paste, hangs a small golden amphora like the one presented by the offerers of the Cerro. The middle row is of similar though larger beads and has six tiny amphorae; the lowest is of globular discoidal beads with hinged gold capsules. This last type appears on jewellery from Galera, Carmona and the Carambolo. As opposed to the above the collars of the Gran Dama del Cerro and of the Osuna flute-player are simple braids.

Belt decorations also show great variety. On the votive offerings some are found to be wide, others striped or braided, and many are decorated with circles, links and brooch-plaques. The type of brooch decorated with interlacing scrolls worn by the Osuna flute-player is frequently found in the cemeteries. Certainly the most beautiful belt-plaques are the four identical ones from a tomb at Verdolay. They are of bronze coated with silver and the central medallion depicts an eagle above another smaller bird—perhaps a pigeon.

Fig. 11

Fig. 12

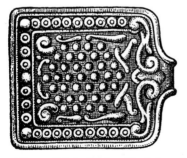

Fig. 11. Belt buckle from Tomb 63 at La Albufereta. 65 mm. × 75 mm. × 8 mm.

Fig. 12. One of four small plaques from El Cabecico del Tesoro de Verdolay, Murcia. 57 mm. × 46 mm.

Characteristic articles of Iberian adornment are brooches and fibulae which are mentioned in the lists of division of spoils among the victors over the peoples of the Tagus regions.

To fasten garments, T-shaped brooches were used, joining two button-holes; they were of bronze, like that of the Gran Dama del Cerro and related to the Celtic ones of the La Tène II period.

Practical utility and beauty were combined in the fibulae. The most common Iberian type was the 'Hispanic annular' one, consisting of ring, pivot and pin, of which numerous examples exist in its simplest form. The type became enriched with multiple patterns and silver inlay and was current among all Hispanic peoples. The Dama de Elche fastens her chiton with a very simple annular brooch, and in other sculptures the fibula secures the cloak on the shoulder. The silver ones from the treasure of Pozoblanco (Córdoba) compete in beauty with the type known as the 'Rider's' in the Celtiberian region. This type (decorated with the forepart of a horse) derives from Eastern art and reached the Peninsula through Greek channels or via the Celtiberian area by Southern Alpine routes.

Plate 59

HOW THEY FOUGHT

The Iberians' martial leanings and their system of warfare are far more apparent to us than their addiction to work. The bellicose nature of the natives was due not only to an innate warlike disposition but also to the poverty of the land and the unequal distribution of wealth which turned those without property into fugitives and outlaws.

Iberian mercenaries already appear at the battle of Himera in 480 B.C. and in 415 Athens considered recruiting them in addition to various others. The people of Syracuse enrolled them as shock troops and Dionysius sent an Iberian contingent to Sparta in 369 B.C. From the year 342 onwards they formed part of the Carthaginian troops alongside Numidians and Celts.

Their numbers, both in the cavalry and infantry, were increased and, according to Plutarch, their particular military asset was their speed. Livy confirms that they 'are accustomed to climb mountains and to leap among the rocks carrying their light weapons'. Neither the Numidian rider nor the Mauretanian lancer sought comparison with the Iberian or the *caetratus*, equal in speed but far stronger. The native form of warfare

Fig. 13

Fig. 13. Horsemen, foot-soldiers and musicians on oenochoe *from Liria*

against the Carthaginians and the Romans was the guerrilla. It was despised by the foe who named this type of skirmishing *concursare*. But, in such uneven terrain, guerrilla warfare allowed a concentration of small contingents and their rapid dispersal at the close of the action.

The system proved ideal for the harrying of the legions and was above all suitable for the Iberians, whose tribal character prevented them from forming strong offensive confederations. Polybius recognized this and makes Scipio, indignant at the treachery of the Ilergetes, speak thus: 'They are no better than bandits who may have some valour for devastating neighbouring fields, burning villages and rustling cattle but who are worth nothing in the army or in regular combat. They will fight with greater faith in flight than in their weapons.'

This was partly true. Scipio must have remembered that the Ilergetes, instead of charging the enemy, started to attack the cattle and that, when the Romans had returned to the coast, the tribal warriors laid waste their allies' fields. They had become bandits, like the men of the city of Astapa (Estepa) who made incursions into the neighbouring fields, capturing soldiers, armed attendants and merchants who had lost their way. Guerrilla warfare and fights between neighbours were second nature to the Iberians and resulted in the systematic sacking of villages and burning of crops. Under such conditions the conquest of Hispania certainly presented a hard task.

Occasionally the Iberians produced chiefs capable of forming strong though short-lived confederations against the foe. Thus Indibil and Mandonius established a regular-looking army in which the various peoples occupied their respective positions— the Ausetani in the centre, the Ilergetes on the right and other *ignobiles* on the left.

Rich and pacific peoples preferred to leave the defence of their territories to mercenaries, as is instanced by the Turdetanians who employed 10,000 Celtiberians in the year 195 B.C. But these proved useless when the Lusitanians devastated Turdetania that same year.

In battle, the warriors were wont to charge uttering war-cries, shaking their locks and leaping as though dancing. Did the infantry give way, the cavalry dismounted, secured their horses and engaged in hand-to-hand combat; the well-trained horses never moved.

The women took no part in the fighting except in the final defence of their land or village. Accounts of violence, collective suicide, burnings and massacres are occasionally of a hair-raising nature.

Cunning in battle was rated equal to speed by the Iberians and they often displayed it. Thus the Hispanic mercenaries of Hannibal, mostly Iberians, crossed the Rhône naked, their garments placed on inflated skins covered with their shields acting as individual boats.

We know a great deal about the Iberians as warriors. Both the written sources and the paintings on pots are lavish in descriptions of their battles. The warriors depicted at Osuna, Verdolay, Archena, Liria and Alloza, as also the votive offerings of the sanctuaries, inform us that the Iberians considered war a noble art. On the 'Vase of the Warriors' from Liria, foot-

THE WARRIOR
AND HIS
WEAPONS

Fig. 14

Fig. 14. *Warrior wearing cuirass and carrying shield and lance (part of the frieze known as the 'Battle between Horsemen and Infantrymen' from Liria)*

soldiers and riders are engaged in combat. Both wear short tunics covered with scaly armour and helmets on their heads; they fight holding shields, javelins and falchions.

Fig. 15   The Romanized warriors from Osuna carry large oval shields like those from Liria or small round ones as well as falchions and broad daggers. On the so-called 'Stone of the Two War-

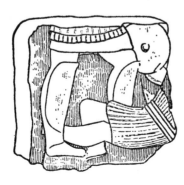

Fig. 15. *Battle between two warriors (from Osuna). Limestone fragment. Length 58 cm., breadth 58 cm., thickness 11 cm. Nat. Arch. Mus., Madrid*

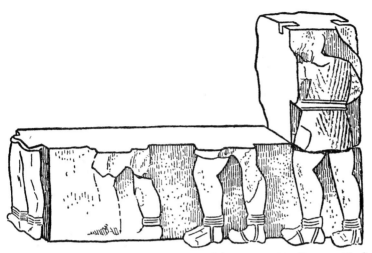

Fig. 16. *Drawing of the 'Frieze of the Warriors' from Osuna. Fine limestone. Total length 1.30 m., height of larger block (in two parts) 72 cm., thickness 25 cm. Nat. Arch. Mus., Madrid*

riors' and in the 'Frieze of the Warriors' are depicted battles apparently between Iberians and Romans or Romanized Iberians. The *acroterion* from Osuna shows a rider wielding a falchion; above his jacket he wears a kind of short *chlamys*.

At El Cabecico del Tesoro de Verdolay was found a vase showing a foot-soldier wearing a cuirass made of strips of metal or leather, with a belt and a short skirt ending in a fringe of strips. Another similar warrior has a crested helmet and, in general, cavalry and infantry carry javelins, round shields and falchions. A small bronze figure of a warrior wears a tunic slit at the skirt and a scaly cuirass; he is armed with a short sheathed sword suspended from a baldric and bears a small discoidal shield. Another wears a cloak fixed to the shoulder by an annular fibula above his tunic and the handle of a falchion is visible. Scenes of battle are depicted on a vase from Alloza between two tribes separated by a river and a vase from Liria shows a river battle in progress.

Fig. 16

Plate 56

Fig. 17

Fig. 18

Fig. 19

77

Fig. 17. Warrior wearing plumed helmet and carry-ing round shield (vase fragment from El Cabecico del Tesoro, Murcia)

The Helmet. Diodorus asserts that the Celtiberians had metal helmets with purple-hued crests, and Appian affirms that the Lusitanians used to shake their long locks in order to scare their enemies. Both wore very similar helmets of metal or of plaited fibre, and the figures of Iberians which appear among the votive offerings of the sanctuaries or in reticulated paintings at Liria have analogous ones. At La Bastida was found a rider with crested helmet resembling one from Despeñaperros, both per-haps influenced by the Archaic Greek type which replaced the conical shape in Greece about the seventh century B.C. Among the various helmets later than the fifth century B.C. in Iberian settlements and cemeteries the convex one from Hoya de Santa Ana and the conical one from Verdolay are wrothy of note. Others of Greek-Etruscan type appear at Villaricos, Alcarace-jos and Quintana Redonda; they lack the chinstrap which, however, is seen on a coin of the third century B.C. from Iliberis.

Some of the Romanized warriors from Osuna have helmets with a long wig and a radial crest of fibres. Others wear bon-nets, tails of horsehair or crests of bronze or leather.

The Shield. When referring to the Lusitanians, Diodorus com-ments: 'In wartime they carry small bucklers of fibre which protect their bodies. They handle them so lightly in battle, whirling them with such skill and speed, that they parry the enemy's blows with them.'

Such circular shields are the kind most common at Liria and Verdolay where their bosses are outlined by dots. This round shield, the *caetra,* was somewhat concave and was worn slant-wise to the shoulder, hanging from a leather strap and held by handstraps. So Strabo reports, and the Turdetanian bronze warriors as well as the Lusitanian stone ones bear him out.

Fig. 20

This type of shield alternates with another larger bossed one, of oblong shape, decorated with geometric patterns, with a long narrow band in relief along the major axis and a broad band along the minor one. The latter appears on the 'Two Warriors' relief at Osuna as also on that of the 'Fighting Warriors' where

Plate 81

Fig. 15

Fig. 18. Battle scene (fragment of large kalathos from Alloza, Teruel)

Fig. 19. River battle on vase from Liria

it contrasts with the round shield of the vanquished warrior. It seems certain that in the first century B.C. the Hispanic peoples used both types indiscriminately, since both appear simultaneously as trophies on a coin of 54 B.C. commemorating victories of 99 B.C. But it is very strange that no oval shield has been found in the Meseta and that, apart from those of Enserune, we only know one boss from Cabrera de Mataro and another from Echarri de Navarra.

Offensive Weapons. The two well-known Iberian types of throwing weapons common to all Hispanic peoples were the javelin (the *falarica* and the *tragula*) and the lance (*soliferreum*).

The javelin was the favourite weapon of the inhabitants of the Levant. Hannibal was wounded by one which Livy described thus: 'Its haft was of firwood of circular section, except at the

Fig. 20. Limestone block depicting warrior bearing a caetra. 65 cm. × 40 cm. × 13 cm. Nat. Arch. Mus., Madrid

tip where the iron was fitted. This was square, like the *pilum*, and surrounded by tow soaked in pitch. The iron was three feet long in order to penetrate both armour and body. But, even if it merely remained stuck in the shield without entering the body, it terrified the foe since it was thrown with the tow already ignited and the trajectory fanned the flames. This obliged the soldier to cast away his buckler and expose himself defenceless to attack.'

From the Celtiberian cemetery of Arcobriga and the Turdetanian one of Almedinilla come socketed javelins with sharpened darts and points measuring $6\frac{1}{2}$ to 14 inches. The earliest known are those from Le Cayla de Mailhac (France) belonging to the sixth century; the type is similar to the oldest ones found at Aguilar de Anguita. Those from Almedinilla are already later in date and pertain to the fourth century B.C.

The *soliferreum* was made entirely of iron with the centre of the shaft thickened; its cross-section was rectangular or hexagonal. The base end was pointed and the long lancehead willow-shaped with bevelled barbs. In some specimens the centre was flattened in order to provide better suspension; the existence of a 'thrower' has been suspected at Liria.

The lance points sometimes reach an extreme length of 22 inches plus another 4 inches for the socket; occasional traces of *niello* occur. A variety of the lance is the *pike*, similar to the cattle-spear of the Andalusian drovers, with a cross at the base of the point, as instanced on a coin of Carisius and a lance from Granada.

Throwing weapons would be useless in hand-to-hand combat, but a picture shows an infantryman with a falchion in one hand and a lance in the other.

The Iberian warrior must have carried two throwing weapons like the *velites* mentioned by Livy; this is borne out by a scene from Alloza. Yet they fought like the Indicetes who, for close fighting, 'discarded the *soliferrea* and the *falaricae* and drew their swords'; or like the Verdolay warrior who defends himself with a lance.

Weapons for Close Fighting. The famed Iberian weapon of antiquity was the curved sabre or *falcata* (*gladius hispaniensis*) which 'cut off arms at the root of the shoulder, severed heads from bodies with a chopping blow, exposed entrails and caused horrible wounds' (Livy).

Its origin is to be found in the Greek *machaira*, introduced into the Peninsula through Etruscan models which must have been imitated by Iberian mercenaries.

The Iberian falchion served for both cutting and thrusting. It was made of a single piece of iron; the blade was widened at the hilt so as to form a support for the *scales* and bent over to guard the hand. In the earliest examples the guard was open; later it was sometimes closed by a bar, a small chain or a leather strip. The pommel ended in the stylized head of a bird, a swan or a horse.

The falchion was encased in a leather sheath with iron frames hung from a baldric. In the damaged stone statue of a warrior at Elche the sheath is held in place by a leather strap and a ring attached to the belt. But, on a figurine from Archena, a sword with bird profile is hung at the belt in the conventional manner.

Of all the Hispanic falchions found in great profusion in the Iberian-Turdetanian area (Almedinilla, Villaricos, Tugia, Cerro de los Santos) and at Archena, Verdolay, Cabrera de Mataro, etc., the most beautiful is one from Almedinilla. The plates and the hilt (which had a sheath of forged ironwork) are decorated with a frieze of plaited and interlaced scrolls between inlaid granules of ivory and horn. The hilt ends in the head of a feline surmounting that of a bird.

Plate 28

At Villaricos, falchions appear with Greek objects dating from the close of the fifth century but they survive until the first century B.C. In the cemetery of El Cigarralejo (Murcia) was found a votive falchion having a horse-head handle of very early type. Other cemeteries of the South and East have yielded more examples but these grow rarer further north. In this last region their place seems to be taken by swords of La Tène II type.

The La Tène II sword, of Celtic ancestry, has its counterpart in the *antenna swords* of the South and Southeast (Villaricos, Illora, Almedinilla and other sites). The oldest known in the Peninsula would appear to be those from Camallera (Catalonia), followed by the ones found in the Meseta (Aguilar, Gormaz) dated to the sixth century B.C.

In the South the swords were accompanied by *antenna daggers* and also by those of 'double globular' type. Their blade is broad and triangular, some 15 inches long and the handguards are right-angled; the oldest date to the fifth century B.C. These daggers originated in Belgium and Burgundy in the Hallstatt C period around the seventh century B.C.

Another weapon was the *falx,* curved and with a shorter blade than that of the sickle. It is seen on late Iberian coins and is found at Puig Castellar (Barcelona) where it dates to somewhere between the fourth and third centuries B.C.

Less well established is the existence of two- and three-pronged spears, despite the fact that Livy mentions their use by the defenders at the siege of the Bastetanian city of Oringis to repulse scaling-ladders. Some spears of this nature have, however, been found at Osuna.

The sling must have proved a deadly weapon and the Balearic slingers, Hannibal's mercenaries, were famous in antiquity. The projectiles of stone, lead or iron occur at Ullastret, Ampurias, Osuna and other sites. Occasionally they were used to despatch written messages.

Standards and emblems must be mentioned as well as weapons. Perhaps every tribe had its own war-cry—we know this was the case with the Lacetani and the Suessetani. The existence of *signa* or *emblemae* belonging to the Iberians is attested shortly after the Roman conquest.

Livy notes that the Romans took 78 military standards from the Suessetani and the Sedetani in the year 200 B.C. Each people used a special emblem; an Iberian coin shows a rider bearing a standard whose staff is crowned with a boar. The Numantian trumpets, like the Spanish Levantine ones of Tivissa, were of baked clay and were used in the manner shown by the Osuna *cornicen*.

We know nothing of the war-chariots, and the only finds of draught-vehicles are carts drawn by oxen-teams (Tivissa, Despeñaperros, Montjuich). A single relief from El Cigarralejo shows a small light chariot but this is most probably a funerary one like that with broken wheels from Toya and another from Alcacer do Sal.

THE RIDER
AND HIS
HORSE

The primitive peoples of Hispania were skilled riders who hunted wild horses in the woods. The Hispanic horse was very like the African, which galloped with rigid neck outstretched and whose course was described as 'deformis'. The profusion of horses in the Peninsula is attested by the vast numbers of riders in the battle contingents and by the exorbitant tributes levied by the Romans.

A great many equestrian representations have appeared in the Andalusian and Spanish Levantine sanctuaries. That of El Cigarralejo in particular was dedicated to the worship of a horse-goddess very like the Epona of the Celts.

The horsemen rode without a saddle; instead, they used a cover of leather, wool or vegetable material called the *ephippion*. Sometimes the padding was extended to cover the horse's neck in order to protect it from the friction of the reins and trappings.

The rider had to manage the reins with one hand and hold his weapons in the other. Nevertheless, some cases exist where the neck-guard becomes a rein-control so as to enable the horseman to use both hands for his weapons.

Stirrups were unknown, but the value of spurs was appreciated; this is shown by the Liria paintings and by the spurs themselves found at Sorba, Mataró, Archena and Collado de los Jardines.

The horse was controlled by means of a halter, a bridle bit and reins. There are vast numbers of bits among the finds and they are in reality more like snaffles acting on the flesh by pressure from front to rear. The so-called 'checks' are simple 'wings' which prevented the sideways movement of the snaffle but put no pressure on the palate.

Plate 26

The Iberians adorned their horses to excess. The pieces joining the reins to the snaffle were decorated with zigzags, S's, dog-tooth and other patterns embroidered or painted on materials or else engraved on leather and metals. The peytrels (or chest-plates) were adorned with fringes of strips ending in bits of tinkling metal. On the crown of the horse's head was placed a sort of parasol decorated with polychrome fibres and this is seen on the horse-collars from Liria and on the mare in the bifacial relief at El Cigarralejo.

Fig. 21

Fig. 21. Horse with 'parasol' over its forehead (vase detail from Liria)

The wings of the bits were composed of rings, crescents or straight pieces with the extremities in the shape of S's. Their simultaneous presence at Tutugi, Liria, El Cigarralejo and other sites robs them of chronological significance.

Much speculation exists as to the manner in which the Iberians sat their horses. They undoubtedly rode astride and yet, because of the position in which some riders are depicted at Archena and Liria, side-saddle has been considered as a possibility. This effect, however, is probably due to the artist's inability to apply true perspective.

Fig. 22

The plastic art of Liria and other sites conveys the impression that the Iberians were an energetic and colourful people with a

Fig. 22. Horseman armed with falchion and surrounded by Iberian inscriptions (from a vase from Liria)

zest for living. They vaunted their prowess in battle, for which they possessed great aptitude, and seized every opportunity to show their mettle.

HOW THEY SPOKE AND WROTE

Our inability to decipher the native pre-Roman alphabets *Fig. 23* —which, despite recent progress, still defy interpretation—is one of the major problems that we face in the field of Iberian linguistics.

Prior to the Roman conquest, various languages were spoken in Iberia. Traces of these lingered on in local dialects and place-names even after the uniformity introduced by Latin. The thesis that present-day Basque derives from Iberian is of ancient origin; consequently, attempts have been made to interpret Iberian in the light of elements it is supposed to have in common with modern Basque. The elimination from the Basque language of Celtic and Latin borrowings has provided a big step forward in Basque-Iberian studies.

Tovar (who has done much research on this subject in recent years) believes that a pure alphabet, the source of the Iberian ones, was introduced in three distinct places and periods. One is represented by the inscriptions (using a syllabic system) found in the Southwest. Another—that of the Southeast—is provided by the Ionic alphabet on the lead pieces from Alcoy and Cigarralejo, as also by the Alicante graffiti. This alphabet was succeeded by the southern and eastern Iberian ones. The third group consists of writing, in the coastal Phoenician alphabet of remote origin, encountered on coins of the second century B.C.

It must also be remembered that the Iberian alphabet was in use at a late period; the Peninsular Celts employed it because the Iberian syllabary was suitable for expressing certain Celtic sounds.

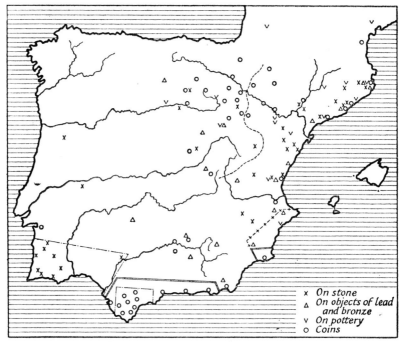

Fig. 23. Distribution of Iberian, Celtic, Tartessian and Phoenician inscriptions (according to Tovar)

THE ALPHABET
OF THE
SOUTHWEST

Fig. 24

The group of inscribed stelae from the Algarve and Western Andalusia may well contribute to our understanding of Tartessian civilization. Although these twenty-odd stelae (inscribed in the so-called 'Tartessian' alphabet) were published last century they are still relatively little known. They have marginal inscriptions in letters of spiraliform tendency and irregular disposition. Their archaeological background is unknown, but they were re-used in cemeteries of the sixth century B.C.

Attempts to decipher them began with Schulten, who assumed a correspondence between this writing and that of the Kamina inscription in Lemnos which is in the Archaic Greek

| Semitic | Greek | M. L. I. | | | | | | | Schulten | Leite | | | | AEA | XXVI | Alcala |
		LXII	LXIII	LXIV	LXIX	LXXI	LXXII	LXXIV	1	AP V	AP XXVII a	AP XXVII b	AP XXVII c	a	113 ff	del Rio MLI LXI
aleph	A	A Δ	A	A	A	A	A	AA	A	A	A	A	A	A	A	R
beth	B							ΕΙ?								
gimmel	Γ					∩			Λ			Λ				Λ
daleth	Δ							A				A				Δ
he	E	‡				‡		‡	‡		‡	‡	‡	‡	‡	‡
wou	F				Ч	Ч	Ч		Ч		Ч	Ч			Ч	Ч
zajin	Z			٦												
heth	H			HΘΧ	H	HΘ	HЧ		ΗΗHЖ		Η			Χ	Η	HH
tet	Θ			Φ				Φ								Φ
jod	I	٧ ٨	٨	٧	٧ ٧		٧	٨	٧	٧	٧	٧		٧	٨	٧	٨
ke	K	K	)I	)I	٧I))	II	II			)I		K			IC
lamed	Λ	1	1			1	1	1			1			1	٢
mem	M								1 Λ							
nun	N	٧ ٢	٧	٧	٧		٢	٧	٧	٧	٧	٧	٧	٢	٧	٢
samech	Ξ	٤						٤	٤ ‡		‡			٤ ‡	∓ ‡ ٤
bjin	O	o	o	o	o	o	o	o	o	o	o	o	o	o		o
pe	Π	٦.				٢	٦								٢
sade	M	M			M		M		M						M
qoph	Q							Χ	Χ						
res	P	٧		٩.	٩	٩	٩٢	٩٩	٩٩	٩	٩	٩	٩	٩	٩	٢
sin	ξ	٤			٤	S	٤		٤	٤					
tau	T							T							X
		‡‡٦				Ϝ						٤	٤		Ϝ
		٨		.					٨						
			*												
						ΥΥ·		٦Γ			ϒϒ	٧			
							~								
								∓							
									≫						
									Φ						Φ
									O						
									٧						
									□			□			
				⋈		⋈		⋈						⋈	⋈
															↑	↑
																D
																⋈

Fig. 24. Comparative table of signs on inscriptions from the Algarve and the Southwest (according to Tovar)

alphabet but in a non-Greek language. This is known as 'Tirsenian' and Schulten's assumption provided the basis for the attribution of a Tirsenian origin for the Tartessians.

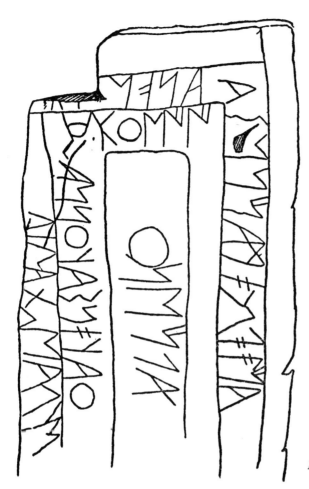

Fig. 25. A Tartessian inscription

Professor Gomez Moreno considers these inscriptions to be the product of a mixed syllabic system with alphabetical signs analogous to the Iberian which derives therefrom. But it seems strange that the Algarve inscriptions should be so uniform whereas the Iberian are extremely varied and lack consistency, thus implying only a brief duration for the system's local development. The main problem lies in determining whether this language was native or whether it was introduced by colonists.

Fig. 25

Two factors seem to favour the latter view. In the first place, this tongue is almost entirely alphabetical (apart from some slight syllabic exceptions) and thus in contrast with the syllabism proper to the Peninsula. An alphabetical system would modify the ancient syllabary and influence the creation or the adaptation of Iberian writing. Secondly, the Tartessian language seems to agree neither with that of Southern Iberia nor with the Spanish Levantine.

Further light is shed on Iberian civilization by native inscriptions in the region between Andalusia and Enserune. Already more than 500 of these, on bronze, lead and pottery, as well as others on coins, are known. From all of them it appears likely that the Iberians of the South and those of the Spanish Levantine-Catalan area spoke dialects of the same language.

THE IBERIAN ALPHABET

The oldest text was discovered in 1922 at La Serreta de Alcoy. It is on lead and the inscription is in the Iberian language, comprising 336 letters of the ancient Ionian alphabet. The same can be said of other texts from El Cigarralejo and Albufereta, as also of two more from Alcoy.

Fig. 26

An inscription written on lead in an alphabet similar to that of Upper Andalusia—the South Iberian—was found at La Bastida de Mogente. Another came from Liria and yet others were painted on pots; these last were written in the Spanish Levantine alphabet. A study of all the known inscriptions enabled Professor Gomez Moreno to establish the Iberian alphabet by identifying five vowels and six continuous consonants and determining the value of the syllabic signs. The only missing factor is the interpretation of certain rarely-used letters.

A difference has been noted between the South Iberian system and the Spanish Levantine-Catalan, especially concerning the signs, but the two have a lot in common. A striking distinction between them, however, is the fact that the southern inscriptions are written from left to right whereas those of the Spanish Levantine-Catalan region run in the reverse direction.

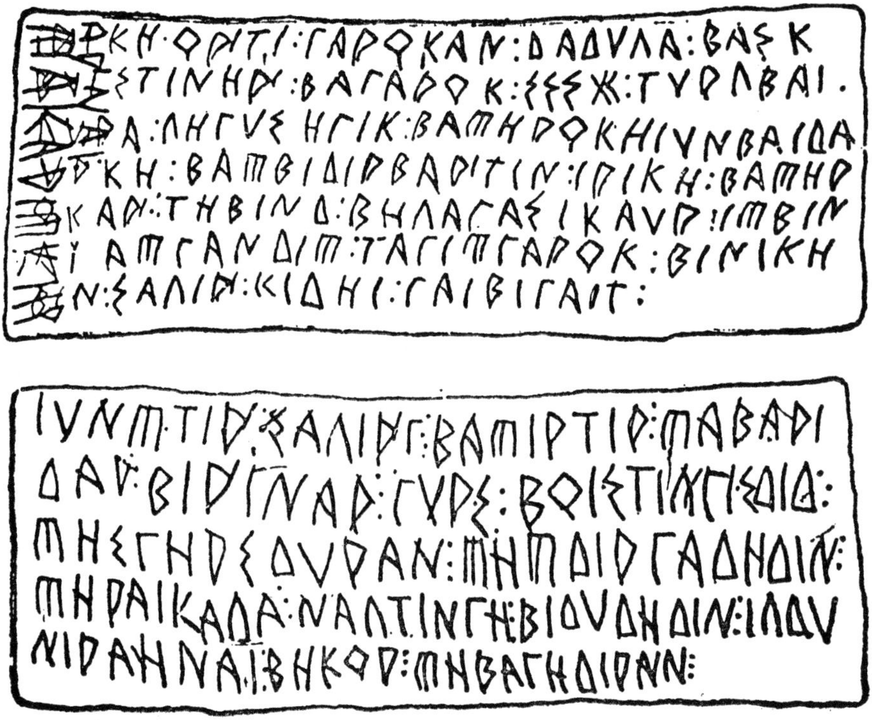

Fig. 26. Inscribed piece of lead from La Serreta de Alcoy (both sides). Length 171 mm., breadth 62 mm., thickness 1 mm.

Those portions of the Iberian alphabet that denote a basic archaic syllabic lettering relate it to the Cretan-Cypriot syllabary (according to Gomez Moreno) and the same applies to the Tartessian alphabet. But Tovar considers that the forms of both these native alphabets are intimately connected with Greek and Phoenician letters. His thesis of the creation of the Iberian alphabet on such bases, 'adapted in accordance with an ingenious evolution and a systematic mind', thus seems feasible. The southern writing appears older, and the Spanish Levantine-Catalan would appear to derive from it since the isoglosses show a basic linguistic uniformity in the area between the Guadalquivir and Ensérune.

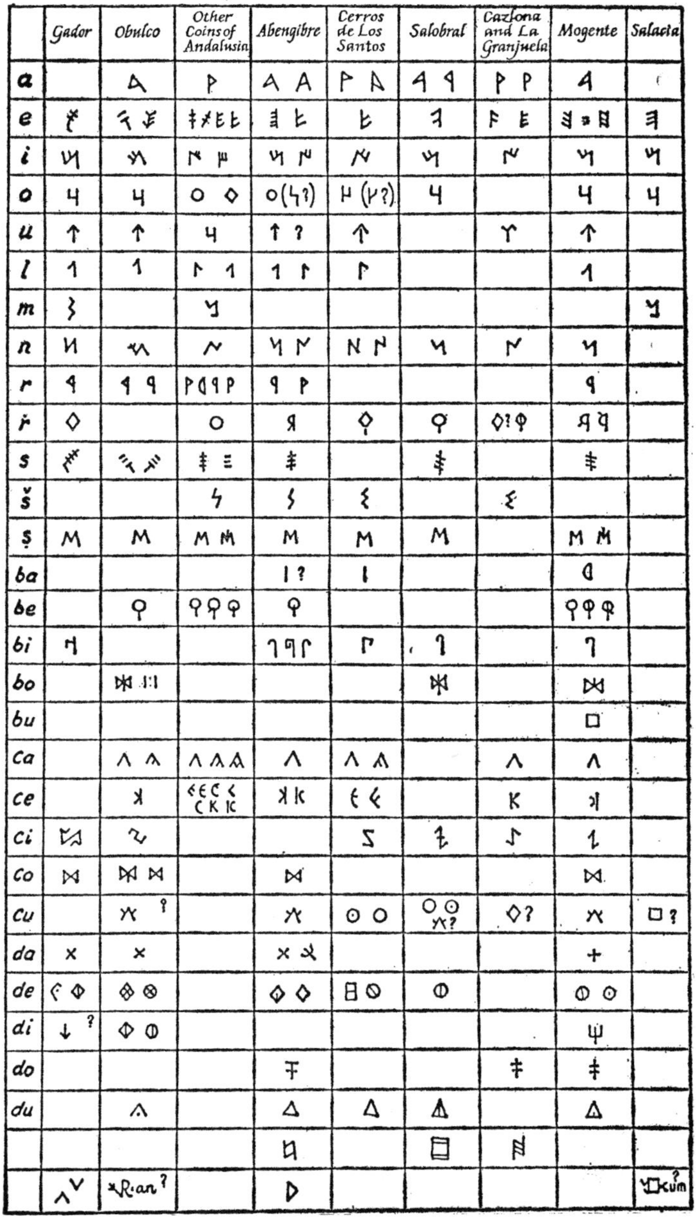

Fig. 27. Signs of the South Iberian alphabet (according to Tovar)

Iberian phonetics are now firmly established, thanks to the above-mentioned lead inscriptions in the Ionian alphabet of the sixth century B.C. They prove that Iberian is totally unrelated to any Indo-European language, including Celtic.

Fig. 27

The southern alphabet agrees with various coin-issues (Obulco, Castulo, etc.), leads (from Gades and Mogente), inscriptions on cherished objects such as vases from Abengibre and La Granjuela and two statues from El Cerro de los Santos and Salobral (Albacete). Inscriptions of this kind are lacking in the region of the Lower Guadalquivir; their absence in this area may be due to the vigour of the colonists' alphabets which drove the native ones into the river's upper reaches.

The nature of the objects on which South Iberian inscriptions occur obliges us to date them no earlier than the fourth century B.C. The Spanish Levantine alphabet also belongs to a late period, since the inscriptions using its letters are mostly found on pottery of the fourth–second centuries B.C.

In the homogeneous group of the Spanish Levantine-Catalan-Languedocian area there are inscriptions whose great import has not been sufficiently stressed.

One group consists of inscriptions on monuments and stelae influenced by the elegant Greek and Roman epigraphy of Ampurias (Santa Perpetua) and related to those on funerary

Plate 80

monuments at Saguntum. Another comprises the Catalan stelae (Badalona, Fraga), perhaps also of a funerary nature, whose decoration proves contact with the Celtiberians of the Meseta. Yet a third group is composed of inscriptions on stelae of Iberianized peoples in the region of Lower Aragon, already influenced by Latin stelae.

As well as the lapidary inscriptions there are those decorating (and perhaps explaining) the scenes on pottery which, in the Liria-Alloza (Teruel) region, are painted but, at Ensérune, are

Fig. 22

scratched. These latter give the potter's name, the contents and capacity of the pot and various other details. From this area also

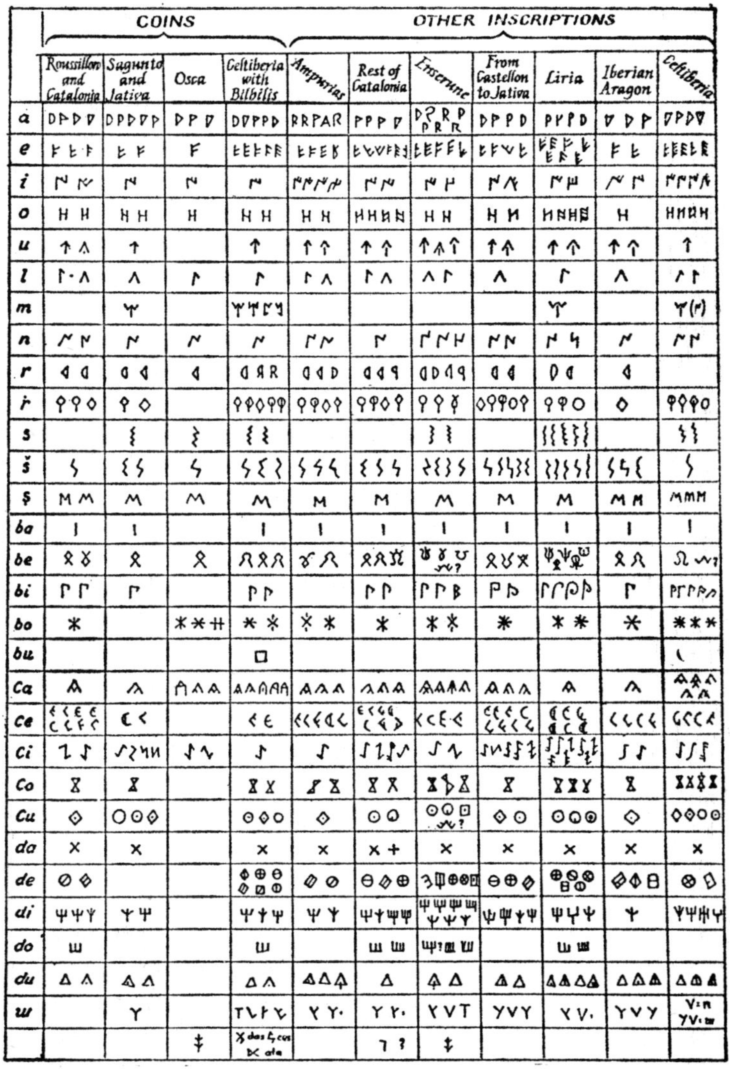
COINS
OTHER INSCRIPTIONS
Roussillon and Catalonia
Sagunto and Jativa
Osca
Celtiberia with Bilbilis
Ampurias
Rest of Catalonia
Enserune
From Castellon to Jativa
Liria
Iberian Aragon
Celtiberia
a
e
i
o
u
l
m
n
r
ŕ
s
š
ṣ
ba
be
bi
bo
bu
Ca
Ce
Ci
Co
Cu
da
de
di
do
du
w

Fig. 28. Signs of the Levantine Iberian alphabet (according to Tovar)

come some pieces of lead inscribed with Iberian letters similar to those of Ampurias. The variety of the inscriptions proves the use of writing to have been widespread and not the sole preserve of a cultural élite.

Fig. 28

The Spanish Levantine-Languedocian alphabet has still many chronological surprises in store. The numerous graffiti of Ensérune, the interesting (albeit scarce) specimens from Ullastret and yet others on small native vessels at Burriach, Arenys de Mar and other sites, prove that the type of alphabet later used on coins was already established in the fourth century B.C. This is of vital import, since Iberian coin patterns (with the exception of imitations of the Ampurian drachmae) did not pre-date the beginning of the second century B.C.

The evolution of the Iberian alphabet from the fourth century B.C. onward is beginning to emerge through comparison of Iberian names in Latin inscriptions with those scratched on imported wares (such as Campanian). The discovery of consonant-reduplication (for instance *n*), the appearance of *m* on graffiti of the third and second centuries B.C. and, above all, the recognition of proper names for specific areas (indicating tribal groups of a certain importance) provide recent evidence of the great benefits still to be derived from studying the Iberian tongue even prior to its decipherment. Some variants of the letters and a lack of consistency in the course of the writing are thought to be the result of the influence exercised by other inscriptions. These confer upon the Iberian script its peculiar archaic character contrasting with outside influences which were Greek in the North and Phoenician in the South.

During the Roman period Latin texts and funerary inscriptions attest the use of Iberian words and their inclusion in names of peoples and places. The 'Ascoli Bronze' which refers to a *turma saluitana,* with more than 40 Iberian names in a specific region, is of great importance. These names consist of a personal *nomen* accompanied by that of the father with the indication of *filius* in a form unlike the Roman and undeclinable.

The existence of an alphabetical system which, with certain exceptions, can be considered as uniform argues convincingly in favour of the cultural unity of the Peninsular Iberian peoples.

Chapter V

Habitation Sites and Houses

THERE IS EVIDENCE that the typical Iberian settlement was an *oppidum* on the summit of an easily defended hill. Livy's statement that more than 120 *populi* submitted to the Romans in the year 217 B.C. must be interpreted as referring to such units. Though the land may have been densely populated and battle contingents numerous, everything tends to make the Iberian settlements appear as mere defensive watch-towers for the protection of the surrounding fields.

Were there any Iberian cities in the true sense of the word? If we take Ullastret to be the Greek Cypsela, then the most technically evolved *oppida* of the Iberian region were Ensérune and Burriach (Cabrera de Mataro). Their architecture was influenced by the Greek settlements of Saint Blaise and Ullastret respectively and, in any case, neither Ensérune nor Burriach provide evidence of being true cities. At a later date, however, one must take into consideration the existence of Gerunda and Ausa which were certainly large Iberian centres. Relations between the various communities of a region lead to a more important type of settlement; this served as the trading centre for a geographically delimited area and possibly also as the headquarters of a tribe.

Fig. 2

We are still far from being able to connect any city or settlement with a tribe or determine any eponymous tribal city. For instance, did Indica give its name to the Indicetes or did it receive its name from them? According to Livy, some of the Indicetes wished to settle close to Emporion and this seems to imply that they founded Indica at a date when the tribe already possessed a name.

What is certain is that, in general, the *oppidum* was a habitation site with a defensive enclosure and that the surrounding

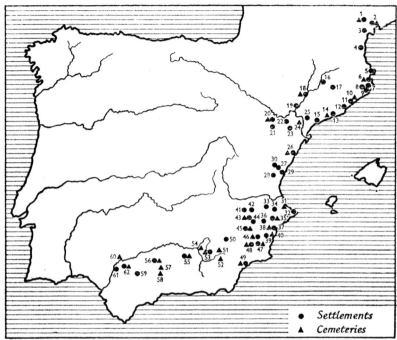

Fig. 29. Distribution of Iberian settlements and cemeteries. 1. Le Cayla de Mailhac. 2. Ensérune. 3. Montlaurès. 4. Ruscino. 5. Rosas. 6. Ampurias. 7. Ullastret. 8. La Creueta. 9. Castell de Palamós. 10. Cabrera de Mataró. 11. Burriach (Cabrils). 12. Puig Castellar. 13. Adarró (Villanueva). 14. Vendrell. 15. Tarragona. 16. Olius. 17. Sorba. 18. La Pedrera de Balaguer. 19. Jebut. 20. Azaila. 21. Alloza. 22. Mazaleón. 23. Calaceite. 24. Coll del Moro de Gandesa. 25. Tivissa. 26. Alcalá de Chisvert. 27. Rochina. 28. Liria. 29. Saguntum. 30. Segorbe. 31. Oliva. 32. Montgo. 33. Mogente (La Bastida). 34. Albaida. 35. Alcoy (El Puig, La Serreta). 36. Villena. 37. Tossal de Manises (Alicante). 38. La Albufereta (Alicante). 39. Elche. 40. El Molar. 41. Amarejo. 42. Meca. 43. Llano de la Consolación. 44. Cerro de los Santos. 45. Hoya de Santa Ana. 46. Archena. 47. Cabecico de Verdolay. 48. El Cigarralejo. 49. Villaricos. 50. El Macalón. 51. Tútugi (Galera). 52. Baza. 53. Castellones de Ceal. 54. Toya (Peal de Becerro). 55. La Guardia. 56. Baena. 57. Fuente Tojar. 58. Almedinilla. 59. Osuna. 60. Setefilla. 61. El Carambolo. 62. Carmona.

plains were cultivated. The settlement distribution map shows that the coastal towns were colonial trading centres—seldom Iberian—with an inland ring of small Iberian forts controlled

Fig. 29

by the towns. The hinterland of Gades, Carthago Nova and Akra-Leuke were within the sphere of Phoenician and Carthaginian influence; that of Emporion (together with Indica, La Creueta, Porqueras and San Juliá de Ramis), that of Hemeroskopeion (including La Serreta, Covalta, Saetabi, Minateda, Albaida and Mogente) and that of Saguntum (as also of Rochina and Segorbe) all bore the stamp of Greek trade.

There are two instances where colonizing influence was so strong that the settlements in question seem truly Greek as opposed to Hellenized Iberian. Excavations at Ullastret are still incomplete but it is evident that there is far more Greek pottery than at other sites—suggesting that it was perhaps a Greek city. The political organization of Saguntum is more akin to that of a Greek colony than to that of a Hellenized native town.

Unfortunately, knowledge concerning Iberian habitation sites is very limited. The main causes of this lack of information are the heavy erosion of the Spanish Levantine conical hills and of those of the steppe-like southeastern regions, as well as the resettlement of the same sites in later times (as instanced in the Guadalquivir valley and the greater part of Catalonia). The lack of spectacular results and the need for systematic excavation campaigns at such sites are yet other reasons why our knowledge of the cities has lagged behind that of the cemeteries. Nevertheless, the splendid defences revealed in some of the towns and the results of recent excavations at others point to Iberian town-planning.

It is convenient to divide our study of the habitation sites into geographical regions in order to understand them better and to relate them with other aspects of life.

Catalonia. In the Catalan region dwelt peoples who can be ascribed to the Iberian complex from the fifth and fourth centuries B.C. To ascertain the location and distribution of the various tribes is difficult, not only because of the vagueness of the texts but also because of the shifting boundaries due to internal strife. Broadly, the distribution was as follows: to the South (Campo de Tarragona) lived the Cossetani who in the third century barred the Ilercaoni-Ilergetes from access to the sea. North of them dwelt the Lacetani and, to the East, the Laietani who occupied the plains up to the coast. Between these plains and the Pyrenees there extended a complex pattern of very backward peoples of the interior: the Suessetani and the Ausetani, and in the Pyrenean valleys, the Bargusi, the Andosini, the Arenosi and the Cerretani. The Indicetes of the Ampurdan were those nearest the sea and their southward extension has been tentatively attributed to pressure exercised by the Volsci-Tectosagi north of the Pyrenees.

In order to establish the origins of the Iberian peoples we must go back to the few Urnfield towns known in this region. That of Marlés represents the type of town plan with oval central area and radially disposed houses the backs of which formed the settlement wall. This type, for instance La Pedrera de Balaguer which has a central street proper to towns of the steppe region, has close parallels in the Ebro valley and in Lower Aragon.

In Iberian times Catalonia had two outstanding though much debated habitation centres: Emporion and Tarragona, both of Cyclopean construction. The problem of dating the walls of Tarragona has not yet been finally solved though recent excavators assign them to the initial period of the Roman conquest in the second century. Very different is the case of Emporion where stratigraphy now suggests a date within the first half of the fourth century B.C. for the wall of Greek Neapolis. Although there is evidence of an older wall of uncertain date, the fourth-century date must coincide with that of the Indicete city or town of Indica. Strabo affirms that Emporion was originally a double city, both Indicete and Greek, divided by a wall. Livy states that both were surrounded by a common wall; the Greek part beside the sea being some 400 paces and the native inland portion 3,000 paces long. The wall of the Indicete centre must have been built in the same Cyclopean technique as the Greek one. This seems to be confirmed by the remains of the enceinte of Indica with its strengthening rectangular towers beneath the Caesarian wall of Ampurias. The fact that Cyclopean construction exists in other towns anterior to the Roman conquest illustrates the strong tradition of this building method among the peoples of the Peninsula.

We know of a great number of towns in Catalonia from the Pyrenees to the Ebro. They are sited on conical heights overlooking the coastal plain and the river lines of communication with the interior. The common plan of these hill-top towns (they are sometimes sited on the slopes) is either that of a grid following the contour lines or of a cone surrounded by a wall. The latter present a very regular plan of squares and both types are widespread in the Catalan region.

The towns of Upper Catalonia belong to the first type and generally coincide with the area of the Indicetes of the Ampurdan and neighbouring regions. Although they are all only partially excavated, it is possible to establish their plan and more especially that of the larger ones.

Three settlements in the region of the Indicetes call for special notice: San Juliá de Ramis, Castell de la Fosca and Ullastret.

San Juliá de Ramis has an area of 70,000 square metres and is one of the largest known Iberian towns. Its rectangular houses, some of them 5 metres long, are built on either side of an axial street. Castell de la Fosca de Palamós, overlooking the sea, is an acropolis on a rocky peninsula with a Hallstatt substratum possessing a natural port and an easily defended isthmus. This ancient town was originally surrounded by a Cyclopean wall. Later it expanded in terraces along the slope and became a fully-fledged Iberian settlement in the fourth and

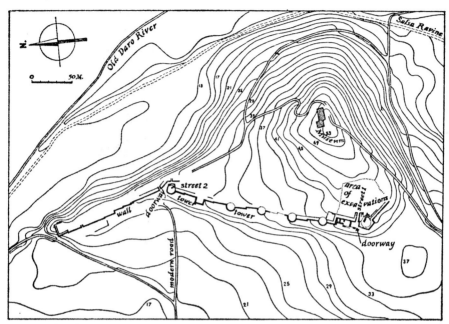

Fig. 30. Plan of the settlement of Ullastret, Gerona

third centuries B.C.—as evidenced by its 'Iberian' wheel-turned and painted pottery. A close parallel is provided by the neighbouring town of La Creueta where living conditions were in all respects similar to those of Castell de la Fosca. Their evolutionary phases are shown by the differences in structure of the various portions of their walls.

But by far the most important settlement of the Ampurdan plain is Ullastret, ranking with Emporion. It is an isolated hill, 30 metres high, above the now dry marshy plain to the south-west of Emporion, close to the sea which formerly lapped its base. It is triangular in shape and covers an area of some 40,000 square metres. On the east side are protecting cliffs whereas the southern and southwestern sides are gentle slopes. To compensate for this, a strong wall 3 metres thick was built around this

Fig. 30

Plates 30–33

part; some 450 metres of it have been uncovered and, in places, it reaches a height of 4 metres. Based on large trapezoidal and rectangular blocks it rises in horizontal ashlar courses whose stones diminish in size as they rise. There are sections consisting of alternating broad and narrow blocks as well as occasional prop stones and grooved wedge stones. All along the wall different building techniques can be observed. Some stretches show only Cyclopean blocks, chisel-chipped in order to reduce their size; this technique of dressed stones is in fact applied practically throughout. The wall was protected by several circular and two rectangular towers situated at intervals of 30 metres.

There are four gateways of which one, the main entrance, has a complex plan and is protected on the right by a circular tower incorporated in a trapezoidal bastion. On the left side the wall bends round to form the entrance passage. This gateway is set back from the general line of defence and later constructions built in front of it concealed its existence. From the gateways ran approaches to the acropolis. The principal one ended in a central area of trapezoidal plan lined with groups of houses, some with porticoes. From another gateway a zig-zag road wound upwards with minor connecting roads at every bend. The excavated houses lie between an *intervallum* of the wall and the acropolis; they are rectangular or square and have many silos dug into the floors of soft rock.

Ullastret, discovered in 1947 and first excavated in 1951, has always been regarded as an Indicete *oppidum*. But it seems to have been as important perhaps a centre as Ampurias, and, for reasons stated above, can be equated with Cypsela. We are still only in a preliminary phase of the study of this most interesting site. Wall sections have not yet been published nor have the various archaeological levels been correlated with the architectural remains. But it seems possible to affirm that the settlement had an ancient wall dating back to the fourth century B.C. This wall was later raised by the addition of rectangular and circular towers perhaps belonging to an intermediate phase. The technique and plan of this wall have parallels in Greek settlements of the Western Mediterranean towards the close of the fourth century—e.g. Capo Soprano de Gela and Saint Blaise.

The architectural details of Ullastret have been given because its technical methods appear to have been copied in some Iberian towns in the Catalan region. These towns evidence a far more advanced type of construction than their neighbours and this can only be explained by the powerful influence of a very important centre such as Ullastret.

The towns of the Maresma coast generally follow the grid plan (Burriach, Caldetas) but the walled cone plan appears at *Fig. 31* Puig Castellar. Burriach is, after Ullastret, the most technically advanced centre. Coigns in portions of the wall indicate the influence of Ullastret on the native builders who also chisel-dressed many of the blocks on their outer surface at both sites. The same influence can be traced at Tivissa (prov. of Tarra-
Plate 70 gona) on the River Ebro in southern Catalonia. Here the entrance was protected by two large towers making up a *Fig. 32* triangular and a rectangular structure with two inner rooms projecting over the wide gap of the doorway—a pattern which reminds one of Ullastret. But, both by plan and siting, this town belongs to those of the regions of Lower Aragon and the Ebro valley with which it was in close contact.

The building material of the Catalan towns was stone; it was used for the bases as well as for the upper portions of the walls. In those sites which have been carefully excavated the presence of adobe (used to top the walls and probably also for other purposes) has been noted. This was the case at Puig Castellar (Sta Coloma de Gramanet) and at La Torre dels Encantats (Caldetas) where small mudbricks of 20 × 10 cm. (similar to those of Martorellas) have also been encountered.

The use of adobe for topping the walls of Catalan towns explains the existence at Ullastret of a large hollow section in the upper parts of the wall nearest the main gateway. This must have served to hold a wooden framework against the stone wall to enable the adobe top and crenellations, similar to those of Capo Soprano (Gela), to be added. Such was the general practice in Eastern Greek cities of the Phocaean area, for instance at Smyrna.

The Ebro Valley. Excavations at the beginning of this century established a group of extremely homogeneous towns in the Ebro valley and in Lower Aragon. They first appeared at the time of the Celtic Urnfield culture and lasted until the phase of late Iberian pottery in the second century B.C.

These towns follow an ancient plan of high platforms enclosed in an oval circle from which radiate houses with two or three wide rectangular rooms usually provided with a portico. The building material consists of large mud bricks (30 × 40 cm.), the use of stone being limited to the low foundations. The Celtic pattern of these plans (either an open square or a wide central street) is obvious. This is confirmed by the basic archaeological material and by some constructional details such as strengthening wooden posts incorporated in the walls (as at Cabezo de Monleón de Caspe), flat roofs sloping towards the front, hearths, side benches and a larder.

As a general rule the oldest towns are those of the Central Ebro area—for instance Cortes and Redal. They contain Hallstatt A elements whose local development in the Lower Aragon region resulted in the fusion of the Urnfield with the Tumulus Culture. Here it is possible to establish three phases of the Hallstatt culture which is eventually replaced by an Iberian phase in most towns. This occurs in the area of the Ilergetes-Edetani peoples: Les Ombries de Calaceite, Els Castellans, Mas de Madalenes de Cretas, San Antonio de Calaceite, etc.

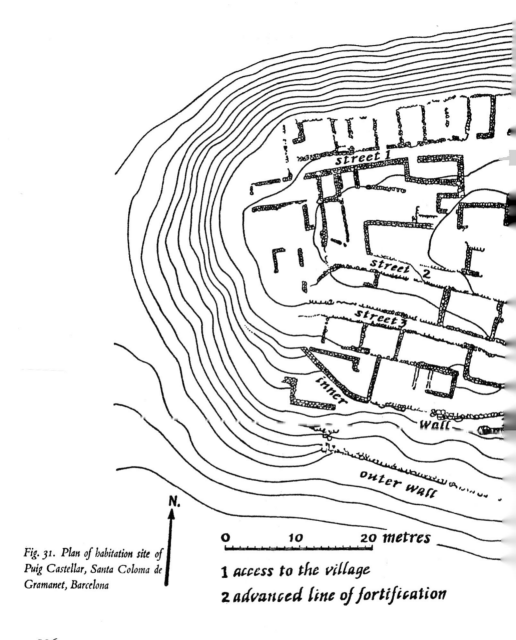

street 1

street 2

street 3

inner wall

outer wall

N.

Fig. 31. Plan of habitation site of Puig Castellar, Santa Coloma de Gramanet, Barcelona

0   10   20 **metres**

1 *access to the village*
2 *advanced line of fortification*

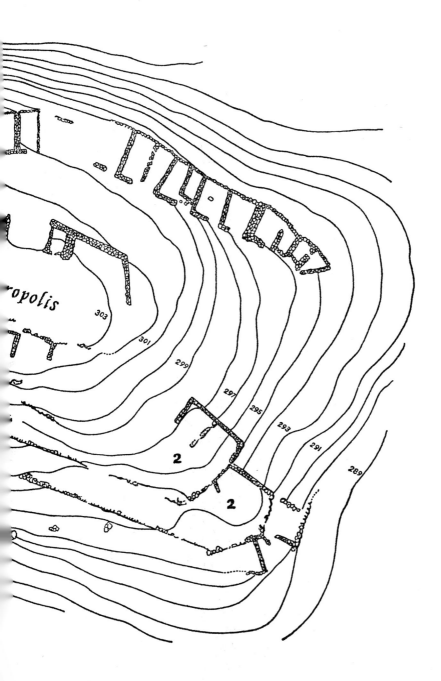

ropolis

303

301

299

297

295

293

291

289

2

2

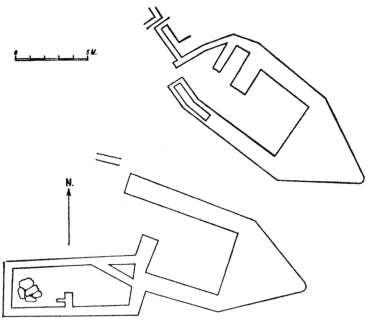

Fig. 32. Plan of entrance towers of the settlement of Tivissa, Tarragona

The earliest towns are Escodines Baixes and Escodines Altes. Iberian pottery first appeared in the fifth–fourth centuries along with improved houses and bigger towns. These events imply an increase of population which tallies with the large armies of the peoples of this area mentioned by the ancient authors. Thus in San Antonio de Calaceite the early Celtic centre situated on the height and belonging to the sixth century B.C. was enlarged towards the end of the fifth. The general plan of a central street was retained, but behind the houses fronting on to it is another rampart road with new houses on the far side. A strange type of house with two opposed apses appears in this town and, in conformity with the street plan, the central houses are larger than those of both extremities. The addition of a wall at the rear must have been motivated by local conflicts at the time of the Iberian invasion of the area. Similar features appear at Les Ombries where smaller houses follow the Iberian pattern, as do those of Els Castellans. At La Gessera de Caseres (Tarragona), rectangular or trapezoidal houses on either side of the central street are surrounded by a wall with rounded corners adapted to the irregular contours of the terrain. The same features are also present at Piuro de Barranc Fondo.

The largest of all the towns in the Ebro region is Cabezo de Alcalá de Azaila (Teruel) which has a basic layer of Hallstatt C–D. It later became an Iberian town and, with various changes, lasted on into the Roman period. Its highly irregular layout of tortuous paved streets agrees in general with that of the central street plan typical of this region. The large rectangular houses form heterogeneous patterns. The wealthier houses have, beside the door, a structure with wall benches of adobe overlaid with lime, similar to those found in the corridors. There are hearths on the left of the doorway and some hollows holding clay jars mark the site of the wine store. The poorer houses have a larder, a granary and storehouses at the farther end of the central room.

La Pedrera de Balaguer (Lérida) illustrates how the Ebro valley towns are connected via the area of the river Segre with those identical ones of the marginal region of the Solsonés: Castellvell, Anseresa and San Miguel de Sorba in the territory of the Lacetani.

In the Iberian town of Castellvell, built above another belonging to the Hallstatt culture, the rocky earth of its house floors had been lowered and levelled and silos had been dug into them to serve as storage pits. Anseresa was walled and its houses were built of stone without the use of adobe. Its floors were paved with sherds—this is also a feature of some towns of the Maresma region, such as Caldetas. A series of circular, oval and rectangular silos, some of them intercommunicating below ground, was noted at Sorba. This profusion of silos is only matched by those of Ullastret and La Fosca where they occur in vast numbers. All these Lacetani towns were destroyed between 198 and 194 B.C. by Cato's raids. Sorba, however, was rebuilt in an attempt to establish friendly relations between victors and vanquished.

The town of Tivissa, 40,000 square metres in area, has a good wall of stone with a Cyclopean base and houses paved with large flat slabs. It was the gateway to the sea for the peoples of the Ebro valley. Its strategic position at the point where the river emerges into the coastal plain was of quite exceptional importance.

The Spanish Levant and the Southeast. The purest Iberian towns, those that lack earlier levels, are to be found in the region of the Spanish Levant. They are usually sited on conical hills close to a river and their plan is a radial grid with raised terraces.

Compared with the paucity of cemeteries the number of settlements is very high in this area. Examples of this type of town are to be found in the hinterland of the plain of Valencia and Alicante, for instance Puig de Alcoy. Another similar town is La Serreta which covers an area of 27,000 square metres. Yet another is Charpolar which guarded the hinterland of Dianium and was itself defended by steep slopes. The most typical and best known of all are La Bastida de Mogente, Liria and Rochina.

La Bastida de Mogente covers some 20,000 square metres and was part of the defensive coastal belt between Hemeroskopeion and Akra Leuke. It was abandoned by the Contestani before the Punic wars began. An untidy group of two hundred houses of complicated plan has been excavated. The finds beneath a thick burnt layer point to the fifth and fourth centuries B.C. as having been the *floruit* of this Hellenized native settlement. In Liria—which may be Edeca—in the hinterland of the Valencian plain, more than 130 houses have been excavated. These are laid out along artificial terraces and the

Fig. 33

finds give a fifth-century date for its inception and the year 76 B.C. for its abrupt end.

Rochina is a different case since its small area of 700 square metres makes it more like a little fort above the river Palancia than a permanent habitation centre. Its 17 rectangular houses lining both sides of a narrow street could not have sheltered more than 200 people. The houses had stone bases, mud brick walls, roofs of branches and floors of beaten earth.

Rochina, Segorbe and other small forts protected the lands behind Saguntum, the great city of the plain. Archaeology is reticent about Saguntum, but Livy gives us a good description of the city at the time of Hannibal's assault. It was attacked at three points in an angle of the wall which projected over a flat open stretch of land. Powerful towers commanded this area and the wall was stronger there than in its other portions. It was built of stones and clay and this explains the ease with which it was demolished by the attackers and rebuilt by the besieged. The *forum,* the last stronghold of Saguntum, had been fortified at the eleventh hour and was sited in the highest sector. The mention of a *forum,* unusual in an Iberian town, the character of its institutions and the parallel offered by its *intervallum* with that of Ullastret, all tend to make us consider Saguntum a true Greek city rather than an Iberian town.

The towns of the Southeast in the provinces of Murcia and Albacete, for instance Meca and Amarejo, are very like those just described. The most interesting is undoubtedly El Cabezo del Tio Pio de Archena (Murcia) situated some 200 metres above the river bed of the Segura and consisting of earthworks and terraces. Its large houses have walls built on a thick foundation of mortar and are still over 2 metres high. In the southern area were found seven contiguous dwellings and on the plateau was a large rectangular construction.

The Upper Guadalquivir. Paradoxically, in this area which was a great commercial and cultural centre as well as being one of

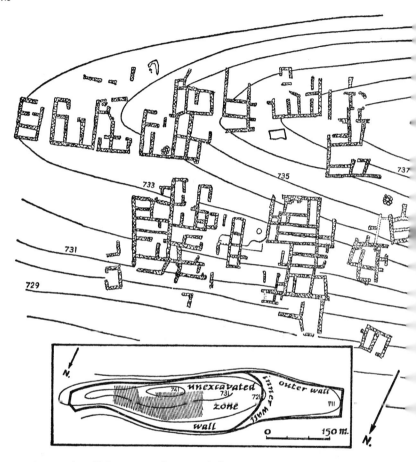

Fig. 33. Plan of habitation site of La Bastida de Mogente, Valencia

the richest in Greek and Iberian finds, we know of only one
settlement site. In contrast to this scarcity of habitation sites
it has yielded a wealth of funerary architecture.

In Iberian times there was a habitation centre close to the
sanctuary of El Collado de los Jardines (Jaén). This was con-
quered by the Romans and its place taken either by a town of
mixed population or by two separate centres. The ruins reveal

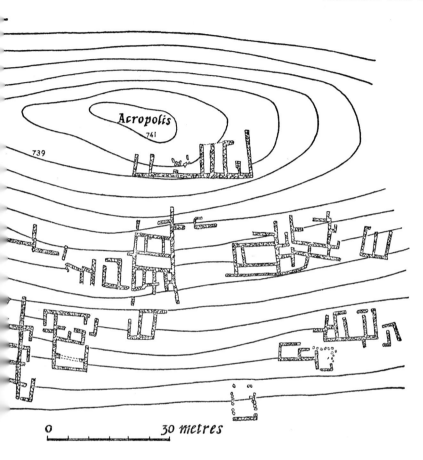

Acropolis
741
739
O ____ 30 *metres*

a large inhabited area of rectangular houses with stone foundations and slate roofs. The walled enclosure forms a talus with
an inner filling of stones. Two towers flank the main gateway
and beyond them a fragment of Cyclopean breastwork is still
visible. Opposite this an angular area had been excavated in
the rock which was possibly a lay-by or else a wider space to
allow room for two passing carts. The houses are in two

separate parts and have floors of beaten earth and tiles of baked clay. Some houses are grouped in threes and fours and it seems likely that certain families used more than one because the larger rectangular houses have two or more entrances. These groups were separated by narrow tortuous streets lacking any set plan.

The Valley of the Guadalquivir. In the region of the plain, the probable site of Tartessos, colonizing activities must undoubtedly have established a certain number of true cities. This would tally with the wealth of finds from this area; but we know of only two settlements, and one of them, Osuna, certainly belongs to the Roman period. The other city is Carmona which, together with the site of El Carambolo, is still in the process of being investigated.

Engel and Paris, in 1903, excavated the fortress of Osuna and uncovered some 100 metres of its wall. This was found to be of hasty construction and its roughly squared blocks were joined together with clay. It has five semicircular towers which provide a possible and interesting parallel to those of the towns in the North, as do also the stretches of the winding wall following the capricious contours of the terrain. This wall consists of two parallel portions facing the talus and having an inner filling of stones and earth. Its date is extremely debatable though local finds suggest the second century B.C.

Carmona is a very different proposition and confronts us with the problem of a civilization antedating the formation of the Iberian culture—namely, Tartessos. This had eluded the earlier efforts of Schulten: his excavations in Cerro del Trigo (Coto de Doña Ana, Cadiz) merely scratched the surface of a Romanized fishermen's town. In El Carambolo and at Carmona the excavators were more interested in studying the stratigraphy of the sites than the plan of the cities. As a result of this policy the areas that have been excavated are comparatively small.

Thus the Andalusian type of Iberian town remains almost unknown. Recent investigations into the relations of the Tartessian civilization with preceding and succeeding cultures have cast no new light on the Iberian world. Nevertheless, these two recent cases of Carmona and El Carambolo illustrate the vast untapped potentialities of the Andalusian area for the future study of the Tartessian–Turdetanian civilizations. The settlements believed to be there—settlements whose importance is implied both by the written sources and the great fertility of the region—await the spade of the archaeologist to uncover them.

CHAPTER VI

Social Life, Trade and Economy

POLITICAL AND SOCIAL INSTITUTIONS

IN THE VALLEY of the Guadalquivir there existed a strong monarchical tradition which the classical writers recalled when dealing with Tartessos. Nowadays it is thought that a centralized power, as perhaps revealed by the megalithic tombs, may have given rise to the Tartessian monarchy. The size and uniformity of the valley favoured such an organization, and the proximity of Southern cities like Gades, with a monarchy of oriental type, would have reinforced it. Another pointer to a central power is the conformity of language attested by a similar alphabet.

The political uniformity of the valley had however vanished before the arrival of the Romans; divided kingdoms, fighting for supremacy, had replaced the ancient monarchy and a centralized economy.

One of the most glaring examples of the Turdetanian monarchs' loss of prestige is that of the *regulus* Culchas who in the year 206 owned twenty-eight *oppida*, but possessed only seventeen in 197 B.C. Around this time we know of other *reguli*, such as Attenes *regulus turdetanorum*, Luxinius 'lord of Carmona and Bardo', and Corribilo *nobilis rex de Licabrum*.

Very often *reguli* were masters of a single city and its surrounding territory; sometimes the same monarch owned two cities whose mutual relations depended on him alone. The title of *regulus* given to these chiefs by the Romans is quite arbitrary; there are occasions when presumably the *reguli* usurped their power from existing legal authority. From autonomous coins of the South we may infer the existence both of magistrates who owed their authority to a king and of those who were elected by the people.

The disintegration of the monarchy is also evidenced by conflicts between various Turdetanian peoples lacking a unified command. A great rising against the Romans, fomented by Culchas and Luxinius, occurred in 196 B.C. and Budar and Besadin are mentioned as *imperatores hispanis* during one of its episodes.

Whether the power was delegated or whether it existed by divine right, it is certain that the southern *reguli* acted as representatives of the cities in whose name they waged wars and contracted alliances. The Romans recognized the lawful existence of the *reguli*, since they accepted submissions by means of pacts with established legal formulae. Scipio proudly declared that he had made real kings of the *reguli* accepted *in fidem*. They had submitted to him in a treaty which promised military aid in exchange for gifts of money, and that implies a negotiated submission and not a surrender of their powers.

The political and economic development of Andalusia explains the Turdetanian social structure. The agrarian wealth of the valley has always resulted from a latifundial system based on exploitation. This implies the existence of a small class of landowners and a huge percentage of paid workers or of slaves.

The merchant classes, enriched through trade with the southern commercial centres, and the ship-owners were component parts of this social pyramid. Long established in the land, they mixed easily with the natives, as instanced by the marriage of Phoenician-Punic men like Hasdrubal and Hannibal with local princesses.

Mining continued to provide a large revenue in Turdetanian times. The private mine-owners swelled the ranks of upper social classes, while large numbers of workers commanded by foremen worked long hours underground. During the Turdetanian period the number of slaves was not as high as it became in Roman times and it seems probable that the majority of the workers were salaried. Inscriptions found in the mining regions indicate the presence of peoples of very diverse provenance.

Owing to hardship among the landless class of the peasants and miners, many quitted their jobs, forming lawless bands which plagued the land. It is thought that Southern society, due to economic distinctions, was divided into castes. These consisted of slaves, landowners, mine-owners and smallholders as well as the important social class of the cattle-breeders.

The Spanish Levant. The Iberian peoples of the Spanish Levant must be considered against a completely different political and social background. The lack of monarchical tradition is explained by the greater remoteness of the Phoenician commercial centres and the geographically difficult internal communications. Greek influence introduced the city-state system of government among these peoples. Here the basic factor was a 'citizenship' of Mediterranean origin which advocated the advantage of the native city to the detriment of all its neighbours.

The result of such a system was a series of small states with a policy favouring local alliances; in the event of confederations they frequently fought against each other. We know the names of some of the *reguli* of the third century B.C.: for instance Edecon related to the city of Edeca and its inhabitants the Edetani. These princes probably possessed executive powers delegated to them by an Assembly or a Senate.

The Ebro Valley. In the Ebro Valley the only people to emerge as a strong unit are the Ilergetes, whose economy favoured cohesion though their hierarchical system had an underlying Celtic bias. Their efforts to form confederations with their neighbours is Celtic in inspiration and corresponds with an expansion of the Celts in the Peninsula at the time of the advent of the Romans. In most cases their *reguli*, such as Amusicus of the Ausetani, were merely military leaders who had usurped power.

The strength of the Senate or Assembly of Saguntum was

due to its Greek origin; its influence on neighbouring peoples is proved by the fact that some of these expelled their petty kings and opted for a Senate. The Senate of Saguntum comprised an aristocratic council but, during Hannibal's siege, this body appointed a *praetor saguntinum* who held provisional powers.

Catalonia. In 195 B.C. Cato summoned the peoples of the Catalan region in the person of *senatores omnium civitatium*, which implies the lack of any body responsible for the task of governing the rest. Ordinary heads of families represented their people within a democratic political system whose uniformity was due to the absence of any vast divisible wealth. This explains why so little is known about the social status of the Northern Iberians as opposed to those from the South.

One of the most curious Hispanic institutions was the *devotio*, recognized by Caesar and regarded as an Iberian custom by Plutarch. It entailed one man pledging total allegiance, by sworn troth, to another considered his superior. Caesar described the practice and noted the obligations of the *soldurii* or *devoti*. These men constituted a personal bodyguard for their chief, shared his sorrows and his joys, defended him on all occasions and never survived him. Viriatus had a cohort of *devoti* who accompanied him on the day of his wedding and on that of his death. This practice accounts for the great number of collective immolations among the Hispanic peoples. The Romans appreciated its advantages and some generals even adapted it to their own use.

ECONOMIC FOUNDATIONS

AGRICULTURE

The Meseta was above all a land of cereals, and it became a rich granary of the Romans. But grain was not the exclusive prerogative of the Meseta: in 203 B.C. when the Romans owned only a coastal strip of the Peninsula, imported Hispanic cereals caused prices on the Roman market to be reduced. The

Ilergetes owed their importance to the wealth of winter grain in the Ebro valley. In Turdetania the lands beside the river 'appeared well cultivated, with groves and plantations of all kinds', while in Lusitania the price of cereals was extremely low in comparison with that of Athens.

Undoubtedly the greatest assets of the Iberians were the vine and the olive, both introduced by the Greeks. The northern limits of the vine stretched from Ampurias to include Languedoc and Provence. According to Martial, Catalan wines, with the exception of those from Tarragona, were of poor quality. In the interior, the vines spread over all Turdetania and reached as far as Carpetania.

The most intensely cultivated region (which also produced the best oil) was that of the Guadalquivir, although, even as early as the second century B.C., olive-trees spread up to the Central Massif in the interior and as far as the region of the Indicetes along the coast.

Fruit trees and market gardens formed a green belt around

Fig. 34. The 'Pomegranate Harvest' (decorated fragment of a kalathos from Liria)

the cities in the same manner as in the present-day *vegas* and

Fig. 34

huertas. Pomegranates, an oriental product, appear on the vase-paintings of Liria, fig-trees flourished at Saguntum, and a great variety of fruit was grown in the South; even the practice of grafting was known and used by these able husbandmen. Pears of the Spanish Levant, truffles of Carthago-Nova, artichokes of Córdoba were renowned; as were also the early roses of Carthago-Nova and the dog-roses of the Laietani.

Flora and cultivation have altered considerably in the Iberian region since pre-Roman times. Deforestation has reduced extensive areas to heaths and steppes. And it is certain that Saguntum, which 'tilled the most fertile region and produced the best fruits of Iberia', did not then grow oranges and lemons; these were introduced by the Moors.

The most admired animal of the Peninsula was the horse, of a similar breed to the Parthian. It was hunted as a wild species in the woods of the interior, and the strength of the native cavalry and the quantity exported bear witness to the great number of horses existing in the Peninsula in Roman times. The she-asses of Celtiberia and the mules of the mountain regions were also famous.

STOCK-RAISING AND FISHING

Though sheep are a natural product of the Meseta, transhumance enabled them to be bred also in the South and in the Ebro valley in the zones of summer grazing between the plains and the highlands.

Hunting wild pig and boar was an Iberian sport, and breeding of the domestic pig provided hams of outstanding quality. The vast quantities of Hispanic oxhides mentioned in trophy lists are evidence of the esteem in which they were held as prizes and also as gifts.

The seas around the Peninsula yielded a most varied assortment of fish. Mackerel and tunny from the Straits of Gibraltar, shellfish from Carteia, murex, octopus and squid, the 'colias' fish from Sexi, oysters of Elche and many other varieties gave

Fig. 35

rise to a prosperous industry of salting and preserving. Sometimes the great cetaceans such as the grampus and the porpoise, and even the whale, appeared in the *Sinus Gaditanus*.

Many of the Peninsular rivers, the Ebro for instance, well deserved their epithet of *pisculentus*.

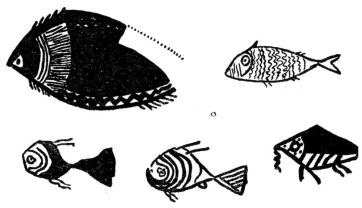

Fig. 35. Fishes depicted on pottery from Liria

Between Tartessos, which had inherited the oldest metal-producing centres, and the tin route of the Cassiterides there extended a trading system based on the wealth of the Iberian mines. The foremost mining region was the Sierra Morena, and the *Saltus Castulonensis* (Castulo, Cazlona) was the hub of the Roman Peninsular policy.

The silver mines of Ilipa (Alcalá del Rio, prov. Seville) and cinnabar mines at Sisapo (Almadén, prov. Jaén) were famous. Kotinai, near Sisapo, was described as 'rich in copper and gold', while Auringis (Asti, Baza) was renowned as a centre of silver smelting. From the time of Hannibal, silver was mined at Acci (Guadix). Forty thousand natives worked in silver mines near Cartagena and a single shaft, that of Baebelo, supplied Hannibal with more than three hundred pounds a day.

Strabo, quoting Posidonius, speaks of the mining lore of the Turdetanians; he mentions their industry in digging deep galleries and their knowledge of Archimedes' screw to remove water.

In the region of Castulo, thanks to the tidal system, ships could reach Córdoba up the Guadalquivir and from there boats made of hollowed tree trunks could go as far as Mons Argentarius.

Some rivers, such as the Genil, produced alluvial sands which were washed and screened for gold, and there were gold mines in the Sierra Nevada where the ore was smelted and purified.

Besides the iron-smelting works of the Moncayo mountain, in the Ebro region, we also know from Livy of the existence of iron and silver mines in the area of the Bergistani and the exploitation of local deposits in other Catalan centres, as for instance Torre dels Encantats (Caldetas, prov. Barcelona), is revealed by their slag-heaps.

To complete the picture of Iberia's wealth of metals we must include the finds of Iberian and Celtic hoards, not to mention the sums levied by the Romans and those extorted by some magistrates. Statistics of the first year of the Roman conquest refer to amounts of gold and silver from regions where mineral extraction is unknown. This leads us to infer intense trade in such regions and the existence of many more workings than are now known.

The highest figure of metal extraction was reached in the year 194 B.C. when M. Porcius Cato carried off to Rome 25,000 pounds of silver ingots, 123,000 pounds stamped with the *biga* (the two-horse chariot), 540 pounds of Iberian drachmae and 1,400 pounds of gold.

The Romans greatly extended the mineral exploitation of Iberia and were eventually obliged to pass laws regarding work and ownership.

INDUSTRY

Plate 43

We also know something of the Iberian textile industry. The profusion of loom-weights and spindle whorls is an indication of its great expansion, and the small relief from La Albufereta of a woman spinning illustrates one of its aspects.

Flax reached Iberia through the agency of the Phoenicians and the Greeks but esparto had long been known. This fibre was most intensively cultivated around Carthago-Nova and, in lesser quantity, in the *Campus Juncarius* in the hinterland of Emporion.

The esparto of Carthago-Nova was long-fibred, and it was used for making rough beds, torches and shoes; Pliny asserts that the shepherds clothed themselves with this fibre. Originally the esparto harvest took place during the summer season but later there was another in winter in order to meet the demand for ships' tackle.

Flax was used to weave fine and beautiful materials. Saguntum, Saetabi, Emporium and, later on, Tarragona specialized in this industry and the last-named was famous for its export of hunting-nets.

Salting and preserving provided a coastal industry; a special type of *garum* (sauce) was prepared from the southern Spanish mackerel.

In addition to household industries such as flour-milling and baking in bread-ovens, the Iberians engaged in the brewing of fermented beverages. The Celts drank beer but the Iberians preferred wine mixed with honey.

CRAFTS AND CRAFTSMEN

Iberian craftsmen excelled in metalwork and specially in the making of weapons. Such was the temper of Iberian swords and daggers, according to Diodorus, that neither helmet, shield nor bone could withstand their blows. Philo attributed their quality to the use of very pure iron and to the practice of working the weapons when cold with light strokes which hardened the blades longitudinally.

The quality of the weapon was tested by grasping the sword pommel in one hand and the blade tip in the other. The weapon was then placed on the head and its two extremities bent downwards until they touched the shoulders: when suddenly released a good sword would straighten out without breaking.

The investigations of H. Sandars and Coghlan do not bear out these reports. The first noted that in a piece cut from the back of the sword the outer part contained carbon to the depth of about one-eighth of an inch; this proportion diminished towards the centre. Coghlan compared a falchion from Almedinilla with an Etruscan one and observed that the latter was far superior, since it consisted of welded soft iron and steel whereas the Iberian specimen was non-vaporized soft iron. The blade was heated in a final annealing operation which produced a magnetite patina. Its raised and recessed decoration presents a problem, for the smith, using traditional methods of forging, might have been expected to obtain the V-shaped pattern by carefully swaging the hot iron and finishing off the work with a file. The blade decoration was, however, executed by a cutting instrument and not by hammering or stamping which would have seemed simpler. Perhaps the sword was a ceremonial weapon and was tempered only for the purpose of acquiring the beautiful blue patina. In actual fact Iberian weapons appear to be but a poor imitation of Etruscan specimens.

The variety of casting of Iberian metalwork will be discussed in a later chapter. Here it is sufficient to remark that repoussé work, niello, granulation, gilding of silver and many other techniques were known to the smiths.

The ceramic industry flourished and many ovens are known where both handmade and wheel-turned pottery was baked, either together or at different times. Knowledge of the wheel, due to contact with the colonists, resulted in specialization. In like manner the decoration of pots by the application of slips and paint must have been the prerogative of workshops; potters' marks and painters' personal stamps give weight to this suggestion.

There was similar specialization in sculpture and it is possible to distinguish styles of local artists, schools and workshops.

From the fourth century B.C. onwards the natives imitated the Phoenician and Greek techniques of fused and moulded glass paste as well as the vase types.

They produced polychrome glass of almost opaque vitreous paste decorated by threads of fused glass applied by means of a spatula. Beads of vitreous paste must also be copies of imports, while another Iberian speciality was pinheads like the one from Cabrera de Mataró.

TRADE

Although little is known of commercial land routes in Iberian times, finds of objects far removed from their place of origin imply the existence of local trade. The presence of foreign merchants is attested by their wares in the entrepôts and by native copies of these objects. Trade among the natives themselves is clearly illustrated by marts and sanctuaries, and the appearance of Celtic objects in Andalusia and of Tartessian gold and silver work in the Meseta is thus partly explained. The treasures of the Sierra Morena, a frontier region between Iberians and Celts, exhibit converging influences of both these peoples as well as that of oriental colonists. These latter were drawn to the vital centres of Villaricos, Tugia, Almedinilla and other sites by reason of the local mineral wealth.

The goldsmiths and silversmiths must have travelled with their finished wares to regions further and further afield, following the demand for their products and their own ambitions. The fame enjoyed by many centres may have attracted orders from distant places and this would account for the presence of vases from Elche and Archena in Ampurias. Similar styles are also found in North Africa and Italy to which *garum* was exported, perhaps contained in the same vessels.

A study of the distribution of local coins is the best way of tracing the economic strength of the Iberian centres. Their distribution indicates the regions economically dependent on the centre of origin which is established by the coin dies.

COINS

From the fifth century B.C. Iberia was divided into zones with different types of coinage representing the spheres of influence of the various centres. Their distribution shows the economic and political status of the country since minting implies political and commercial independence backed by a supporting power.

Massiliot coin-types (Auriol type) are the earliest known in GREEK COINAGE Iberia but around 450 B.C. there began to appear at Emporion small uninscribed silver coins, symbols of the city's economic and political independence. Later, fractions of the Massiliot drachma, minted at Emporion, were distributed as far afield as Cape Nao. At the start of the fourth century, Rhode (Rosas) also minted coins; the drachmae of Emporion, bearing a nymph and a horse, indicate Punic influence.

Towards the close of the same century, Rhode struck drachmae depicting a rose whereas Emporion minted drachmae and fractions thereof stamped with Pegasus and, later, with Chrysaor; these lasted until the period of the denarius and included coins of debased type.

Greek coins of Emporion are found in the area between Massilia and Carthago-Nova; they were very important because they provided the basis of all the native series. The coinage of the Iberian cities minting silver coins of Greek type but with Iberian inscriptions attest this pre-eminence of Emporion.

IBERIAN
COINAGE

Plates 87–89

Plate 83

All Iberian coin-types are readily recognizable; they all bear a rider with a palm or a weapon (lance, *falcata* or *falx*). Their distribution covered a wider field than did Iberian pottery; they reached the Celtic Meseta where the Iberian coinage alphabet was used and the types were copied in the local style.

The chronology of Iberian coins begins with silver drachmae imitating those of Emporion about 180 B.C. One of these imitations is the bronze as minted at Indica, bearing the head of Pallas, a Pegasus and the Iberian legend Undi-ce-s-cen. The coins representing fractions carry various animals on the reverse and some series indicate possible values and the names of magistrates.

In the twin city of Arse-Saguntum, before 219 B.C., were minted silver coins among which may have been one bearing a head of Diana and, on the reverse, the inscription Arse-s-cen between the spokes of a wheel.

Plate 82

From the year 180, large and well-made coins appear at Cese (Tarraco), Saguntum, Ildirda (Lérida), Ausescen (Vich) and other sites.

Plates 84–86

The minting of silver coins and of denarii reached its peak in the last quarter of the second century B.C. During the Sertorian wars, around 83 B.C., special bilingual coins were minted. Issues bearing Iberian inscriptions ceased in 45 B.C. and were replaced by Hispanic-Latin coins although some of the earlier types continued to be used.

Various commercial centres of the Languedoc minted coins with Iberian inscriptions and designs, for example Nero (Narbonne), Seloncen (Ensérune) and Brigantin. The number of native trading centres during the period between the third and first centuries B.C. implies a self-sufficient and decentralized economy. Some coins appear at a great distance from their place of issue, thus attesting the commercial scope of centres such as Cese, Indica and Arse.

Among the Andalusian coins the following groups can be distinguished thanks to the alphabets of their inscriptions.

COINAGE OF ANDALUSIA

Plate 85a

Between Almeria and Huelva coins have been found bearing inscriptions in identical letters, peculiar to Andalusia, for instance, Orke (Urci, in Almeria), Ikalosken and Castulo in the province of Jaén. Others of more advanced type carry abbreviations of magistrates' names, e.g. Ildiberga, Obulco. These coins appear to have lasted until the Augustan period and bear Latin and native bilingual inscriptions.

The coins of the Phoenician entrepôts of the South— Villaricos, Gades—and Ebussus (Ibiza) are hard to date because they continued into Roman times bearing the same Phoenician inscriptions. The oldest coins with the widest distribution are those of Gades stamped with a Hercules, tunny fish and dolphins, and those of Ebussus which bear a cabirus and lasted until the reign of Caligula.

Punic silver and bronze coins of the Barquidae period appear in the South between 239–205 B.C. Their series are of excellent quality and they were practically all minted in Carthago-Nova.

Between the Serranía de Ronda and the sea, coins with inscriptions in Libyan-Phoenician, Latin or bilingual texts were minted during the second and first centuries B.C. at Acinipo (Ronda), Bailo (Bolonia), Lascut, Iptuci and other centres.

Coin distribution between the fifth and first centuries B.C. indicates that the economy of the Spanish Levant and Catalonia was based on the Ampurian drachma whereas the entire South was under the sway of Punic entrepôts. Nevertheless, the autonomous economic peak of the Iberian commercial centres was reached during the third and second centuries B.C.—a fact which agrees with other observations in the field of Iberian studies.

CHAPTER VII

Religion and Ritual

RELIGIOUS BELIEFS

RECENT STUDIES have established that Iberian religion was Mediterranean in both belief and ritual. Avienus mentions astral, solar and lunar cults in islands and on capes; symbols of moons, crescents and stars on Iberian reliefs and coins point to the same ideology.

More than 200 Roman inscriptions to native deities are known, all from the Meseta and the Northwest. Lack of a Celtic alphabet explains the existence of such Latin inscriptions on tombstones of a late Roman period. The rapid Romanization of the Iberians must have destroyed the native cults. Our inability to decipher the Iberian alphabet renders anonymous many deities whose names probably appear on Iberian inscriptions.

Possibly the names of gods so preserved in Roman inscriptions originated in a pre-Celtic substratum to which would belong the divinities of the sanctuaries mentioned in the *Periplus*.

Other coastal sites possessed sanctuaries dedicated to a marine goddess of the Astarte-Venus type. This seems to indicate a system of assimilation as testified by the temples of Gades and Villaricos, the statues of Tanit, and the temples of Cronus-Moloch and Melkart at Gades served by priests in the eastern manner. The statuette of Demeter found in the tomb of Galera has its prototypes at Haghia Eirene (Cyprus) and Solunto (Sicily) and illustrates the oriental nature of the religion which permeated Turdetanian society.

Plate 21

The cult of the bull has an ancient Mediterranean origin. In the Peninsula, where it can be traced back to the time of Geryon, it is symbolized by the heads found in the Balearic (Costitx) and Andalusian sanctuaries.

Fig. 36. The 'Winged Goddess' (pottery fragment from Elche)

Plate 39

Dove-worship, in which the dove personifies the Mother-Goddess of fertility and priestesses and offerers present the birds to the divinity, seems parallel with the bull cult.

The same Mediterranean idea is symbolized by the great number of lions, monsters, sphinxes and other animals, and by the Spanish Levantine sanctuaries related to the Ephesian Artemis, Zeus and Cronus-Saturn.

Plate 67

Fig. 36

The winged goddesses of the Elche pottery are attributed to Hellenic tradition, as are also the reliefs of Pothnia Theron and Pothnia Hyppon and the scenes of the Tivissa *phiale*. The female tamer of Elche is depicted among rampant horses, and the scene was inspired by a relief from temple B of Prinias dated to the end of the seventh century B.C. and in another from Arkades in Crete. The same divinity appears on the ear-rings of Santiago de la Espada. Her masculine counterpart is to be seen on many different reliefs, mostly in the Iberian area

Plate 42

(Villaricos, Saguntum, Mogón and Balones) although he also exists in the Celtic region.

The sanctuary of El Cigarralejo was also dedicated to Pothnia Hyppon, whose torso was found beside a hand holding doves. Some of the goddesses of Elche and one of Santiago de la Espada are related to the prototype found in the sanctuary of Arthemis Orthia of Sparta.

The blending of Mediterranean and Celtic religious ideology is illustrated by the 'Carriazo bronze' which depicts a deity springing from the union of two birds and holding a triangle in either hand. This figure is interpreted as the goddess of fertility derived from the identification of Hathor with Isis; the triangles are a schematization of the lotus flower and the birds represent the Celtic solar ship. The blending of the two elements must have occurred in a contact zone, perhaps Tartessos, which would explain the Eastern symbols of the Carmona ivories, the cauldrons with griffins, and the griffin above a lotus of the Aliseda belt to which we shall return later (*see* pp. 180 f.) as well as the similar ones from Cerro de Berrueco (prov. of Salamanca) and from Sanchorreja (prov. of Avila). In this last example, as in the Ibiza plaque, dated to between 650 and 600 B.C., the sacred tree has taken the place of the goddess. This is the selfsame tree that appears on the painted pottery from Azaila and on a plaque from Despeñaperros.

The Tivissa *phiale* is of great importance for the understanding of Iberian religion. It is of silver gilt and has a lion's head soldered in its centre; around this are depicted various scenes engraved with a chisel. The outstanding one represents an infernal divinity (Hades) to whom someone is offering the symbol of immortality, a centaur—son of the Earth—a huddled figure like the ones on the Tomb of the Harpies of Xanthos, a wild cat and some wild boars. A second group comprises three daemons (very like the Etruscan *lase*), one of whom is sacrificing a sheep while another collects its blood and the third bears a tripod scent-burner. Iberian parallels to this scene are provided by a ring from Tivissa, the Elche vase-paintings,

Plate 27

Plate 2

Plate 74

Fig. 37

Fig. 37. Symbolic cult scenes (from the Tivissa patera)

and the ear-rings of Santiago de la Espada. A third scene shows a rider with a lance and shield galloping towards a lion which is devouring a wild boar. The funerary symbolism of the hunting scene is clear, as is also the infernal nature of the lion's head at the centre of the *phiale*.

In other Iberian *paterae* from Tivissa, Perotitos, Toya, etc. there is a central *gorgoneion* which has direct prototypes in Ras Shamra and Crete. Despite its Eastern origin and influence the *phiale* of Tivissa is considered a native creation which can be dated to between the fourth century B.C. and the beginning of the second, when the town was destroyed.

We know some sacred places in the South and the Spanish Levant where nature-worship must have prevailed over concrete forms of anthropomorphic religion. These places were habitation centres; their purpose was manifold and they served religious, political, social and artistic ends.

That these sanctuaries attracted pilgrims explains the presence of votive offerings artistically distinct from the official sanctuary style. Even more than a temple the place was a treasure house (*thesauros*) for storing the offerings of the faithful, and maybe the offering *Damas* were not priestesses but princesses attired for the ceremony.

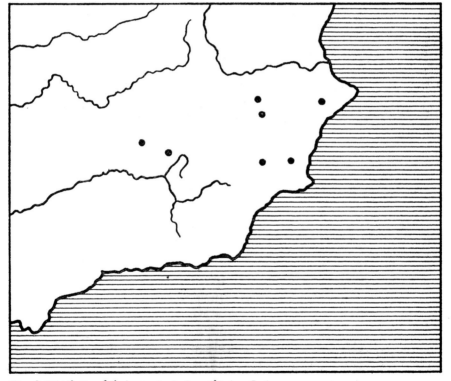

Fig. 38. Distribution of Iberian sanctuaries in southeastern Spain

The offerings were fruits of the earth: bread, oil, hydromel, and especially votive representations by means of which the believer sought to perpetuate his image before the god whose aid he solicited. Since this was a naturalistic religion its ends were health for the village from Nature and for the whole community through Man.

The sanctuaries must have been set in places where the natural conditions were considered suitable for divine apparitions. Some are found on eminences, others close to caves, in craggy surroundings or near a spring. The ceremonies must have been basically of a political nature, and the destruction of these centres of resistance and nationalism proved essential to the conquerors. Almost all were totally or partially destroyed during Hannibal's campaigns; it would appear that the Romans adopted a more gentle policy of conciliation.

Among the Andalusian sanctuaries the most famous, by reason of their many bronze votive offerings, are those of El Collado de los Jardines (Santa Elena, prov. of Jaén) and Castillar de Santisteban in the same province. The first site comprised two superimposed temples built on artificial terraces. The first sanctuary was destroyed during Hannibal's campaigns and the second, built on its ruins, lasted until the Roman period.

Castillar is an enormous rock-shelter with a rock-cut terrace and steps in front of which the offerings were found. The nature of the votive offerings relates this site with the sanctuary of Nuestra Señora de la Luz (Murcia). The sacred area is a raised terrace situated between ravines and containing dwellings we associate with the third century B.C.

El Cerro de los Santos and El Llano de la Consolación (Montealegre, prov. of Albacete), both of which were characterized by large stone sculptures of *Oferentes* (bringers of gifts), constitute another group. The first contained the remains of a large rectangular *thesauros* with a big front portico like a temple *in antis*; two Ionian capitals show the original structure to date from the fifth century B.C. El Llano de la Consolación offers a variety of elements such as fragments of Iberian-Greek cornices, Ionian capitals and large sculptures.

The sanctuary of El Cigarralejo (Mula, prov. of Murcia) has recently been excavated. A group of dwellings was found within the acropolis, and in one of them (at a lower level where lay the ancient part of the sanctuary) were the votive offerings. The oldest portion of the site is of the fifth century B.C. and it endured until the wars of Hannibal when it was destroyed and rebuilt. This new sanctuary in turn disappeared in the second century B.C. and was replaced by a Romanized settlement. A peculiar feature of this site is the almost exclusively equine nature of the votive offerings, implying the worship of a goddess who was protectress of horses.

Plate 34

Further north another sanctuary is known, that of La Serreta de Alcoy (province of Alicante), where the sacred area can be identified by a destroyed building of the settlement. The votive terracottas are of Punic type as at other sites within the Spanish Levantine-Catalan area, for example at Sidamunt (prov. of Lérida). The sanctuary was in use during the Roman period but life in the early nucleus was governed by Punic influences, as in Ibiza whose art is closely related to that of La Serreta. In general, it has been possible to date the sanctuaries by their styles of sculpture and pottery. The majority lasted until Roman times but the initial phases of some can be traced back to the fifth century B.C.

LIFE AFTER DEATH

At the start of this century the tombs of the Iberian area and the Celtic ones of the Meseta were grouped together, on the strength of the typology of their grave goods and the similarity of their rites. This has since changed; scientific excavations and

FUNERARY
RITUAL

the discovery of Iberian objects within the Celtic cultural area and vice versa has widened our horizon.

The basic element of the Iberian funerary rite of cremation was adopted from the Urnfield culture but with Eastern Mediterranean influences. It was customary to bury the ashes in an urn and to lay it in a hollow in the earth (*loculus*), surrounded by grave goods and offerings. The graves are disposed haphazardly as opposed to those of the Meseta which are laid out in rows. But there are many variations; in Andalusia, for example, a tumulus is erected over the grave. It is possible that these Andalusian tumulus-graves represent the Pantheon of Tartessian-Turdetanian royalty.

Cremation took place in funeral pyres outside the tombs (*ustrina*); later, the ashes were gathered and placed in the urn, which was then set on benches or in niches and trenches within the chambers along with the offerings. The fact that broken wheels have been found in some Andalusian tombs, and that human remains are sometimes lacking, does not mean that the corpse was inhumed or that it was borne there on a funeral chariot; the wheels are part of dismantled carts which were offerings to the departed. Once the urn and the grave goods had been put into place, the entrance was sealed in a manner which would allow the chamber to be reopened for further burials.

Ancient texts make mention of various funerary practices among peoples of the South, especially those of the Lusitanians. On the death of the chief Viriatus, his corpse, attired in his finest raiments and with his weapons at his side, was burnt on a tall pyre. Immediately this was kindled the warriors began a frenzied dance around it, while squadrons of horsemen executed funerary marches. The bards sang of the glorious deeds of the dead hero and, later, when the flames had died down, there were funerary games comprising 200 paired contests above the grave.

The funeral ceremonies of lesser men were probably of a simpler nature. Weapons and offerings were usually burnt and later placed either in the urn or around it. *Falcatae* were for the most part bent double and *soliferrea* twisted, as were javelins and heavy weapons, while helmets were dented to prevent re-use or desecration.

Some reiterative Iberian inscriptions may have been magic formulae to stave off all evil from the dead and to call down a curse upon tomb-robbers. The only known *stelae* in the Iberian area are a *baetyl* from la Pedrera de Balaguer and the rough *stelae* marking the graves found in Ensérune.

Southern France and Catalonia. Towards the middle of the first millennium two funerary rites co-existed in southern France, inhumation and cremation, respectively representing both stages of La Tène culture. The two key cemeteries of the area of the Midi are Cayla de Mailhac (Aude) and Ensérune (Hérault).

At Cayla there is a series of cemeteries corresponding to different phases of the settlement between 750 and the fifth century B.C. That of Moulin (750–650 B.C.) is a typical Hallstatt type urnfield, and that of Le Grand Bassin I (650–550) still belongs to the native period previous to Greek contacts. Urns were used for burial and each grave represents an ossuary. Grand Bassin II (550–475 B.C.) already has Attic imports and the funerary ritual is different: burial is now in a cavity (*loculus*) of the size of the urn which is covered with ashes and coals. Grave goods are few, and their presence distinguishes 'warrior tombs' with an urn and offerings from the poorer graves occasionally lacking an urn and having only the burnt bones within the hole.

The cemetery of Ensérune II carries the chronology of Cayla a stage further and illustrates the differences in ritual. The first stage (*c.* 425–325 B.C.) has two forms of urn burial in *loculi* with red-figured Attic vases of 360–325 B.C. or else in an urn with practically no pottery. Phase II, from 325 B.C. to 220 B.C.,

CEMETERIES
AND GRAVES

Fig. 29

139

follows a ritual proper to the late urnfields with La Tène II
offerings; the ossuary is either a South Italian *krater* or a
blackish and grey urn decorated with geometric patterns of
supposed Celtic origin.

These two cemeteries of the Languedoc are extremely important for the understanding of ritual in the Catalan area since
the identical forms recur in that region. The native cemeteries
of Emporion (Parrallí and that of the Northeast Wall)
illustrate the same sequence as at Cayla. The cemetery of
Parrallí is an urnfield of the type of Grand Bassin I and
Agullana. The next stage is illustrated by that of the Northeast
Wall analogous to Grand Bassin II, with Attic imports; the
urns are found in *loculi* of burnt earth. It is significant that
occasional inhumations occur in this cemetery, since the Greek
graves of Portitxol are supposed to belong to the Palaiápolis
(*c.* 580 B.C.). Some cremation graves of the Martí cemetery,
also at Emporion, surrounded by others containing inhumations and Greek objects, are thought to be native. The lack of
ritual uniformity in these cemeteries suggests a social as opposed
to an ethnic differentiation, but this is a matter of conjecture.

The Catalan parallel to Ensérune II is seen at Cabrera de
Mataró (prov. of Barcelona). Here the graves formed scattered
groups, each comprising two funerary urns, some of which
were South Italian *kraters*, with offerings which consisted of
plates with remains of food, birds' eggs, sea shells, fish bones,
egg shells and so forth. Weapons bearing traces of burning
were found beside the urns. This cemetery of the Laietani is
dated to between 350 and 300 B.C.

Further south, a recently discovered cemetery at Vendrell
(prov. of Tarragona) contains scarabs belonging to the beginning of the fifth century B.C. The grave of Coll del Moro,
which appears to have had a tumulus, illustrates Celtic and
Graeco-Punic influences on the traditional and local form of
the urnfields. The inhumation burial of Coll del Moro, dated

by an Attic *kylix* of the fourth century B.C. and 'proto-Iberian' pottery, must be related to those of Lower Aragon, which contain urns.

A like background is found at the cemeteries of La Pedrera de Balaguer in the province of Lérida. The little we know of them suggests phases corresponding with those of the settlement from the eighth century B.C. onwards. The rite of cremation lasted until the appearance of wheel-turned pottery between the fifth and second centuries B.C. The cemetery corresponding with the Iberian phase has yielded a rich collection of grave goods comprising pots, weapons, helmets and bridle bits. Perhaps the horse-burials in the graves belong to this stage; some are of horses only with no traces of the riders, but two graves each contain two horses, and their bronze head-pieces are like those found in Gaulish and Etruscan chariot-graves.

The Ebro Valley. Apart from La Pedrera, there is no known cemetery of the Iberian stage. The known cemeteries of Lower Aragon are derived from the *Hugelgräberkultur*; the earliest phase is represented by Roquizal del Rullo (Hallstatt C–D) and the latest by San Cristobal de Mazaleón. The majority of the graves are cremation tumuli enclosed by a rough circular wall, with rectangular stone cists containing the urn. Over the cist was a stone filling and the whole was covered by a tumulus of earth and stones. Sometimes there were small, even stone slabs above the cists—as at the cemetery of Azaila. On other occasions the cist was of large proportions (as at San Cristobal de Mazaleón), and yet another variant was a cist beneath a tumulus having a retaining circle of large orthostats (Cabezo de Monleón de Caspe).

The earliest type seems to be the stone slab cist from which derive the masonry-walled cist of Mas de Flandi. The common prototype is very ancient despite the fact that Urnfield rites lasted until the Iberian period at Azaila.

The Spanish Levant. Only one cemetery, that of Oliva in the province of Valencia, is known in the area ascribed to the Bastetani and the Edetani. The cremation graves include two types of urns, hand-made Celtic and wheel-turned Iberian ones. In this cemetery, shapes derived from the urnfields and from the excised pottery tradition continued in use, as well as belt-buckles and Hallstatt fibulae. We appear to be dealing with Celtic infiltrations from Lower Aragon and a late retarded phase of the Iberian. As opposed to this, the urnfields of El Boverot (Almazora) and Els Espleters (prov. of Castellón) seem to come to an end before the Iberian occupation.

The cemeteries of La Albufereta and El Molar are situated in the province of Alicante, the area of the Contestani. In the first-named, which begins in the fifth century B.C., cremation followed an original pattern. The corpse was burnt in a vertical position inside a well whose fire was fed by air through pottery pipes reaching to the bottom of the shaft. A layer of ochre and shells was strewn above an earth layer, beneath which lay the urns, propped by stones and covered by small flagstones. Among the grave goods are to be noted the typical *braserillos* and some weapons related to those of Meseta type.

The Southeast. The cemeteries of Murcia and Albacete form a homogeneous group recently excavated; this has proved of great value in dating the Iberian art of those regions. The cemeteries of Llano de la Consolación, Hoya de Santa Ana, Cigarralejo and Cabecico del Tesoro de Verdolay have provided numerous native sculptures which belonged to the Deitani and the Contestani.

At Llano de la Consolación the cemetery of La Viña de Marisparza has been explored and its cremation graves have yielded Iberian warriors' grave goods and Attic pottery of the fifth–fourth century B.C. This site and some others, as for instance El Cigarralejo, are characterized by tumuli with rectangular paving above the urns. The graves are found beneath, around and above the tumulus, thus demonstrating the different phases of the tomb's use. In one was found a funerary urn together with a *kylix* of the fourth century B.C.; a similar vessel lay above the paving, while other urns and Iberian pots with linear decoration were disposed around.

More than 300 graves covering a period between the fifth century B.C. and the Roman Empire were found at Hoya de Santa Ana. Besides tombs similar to those just described, there were isolated urns in *loculi* containing the ashes and the grave goods. In one instance the burial and the funerary offerings were laid on the same pyre (*bustum*) of almond wood ashes and the whole was covered by large stone blocks.

Among the notable finds made there were the 'Vase of the Dragons', small bone plaques with swastikas, meanders and lotus flowers, and a vase decorated with hollow silver bead-work together with various *omphaloi*.

At El Cigarralejo the urns lay in hollows, sometimes under oval or rectangular paved tumuli. These urns are either Iberian or of Celtic ancestry, like the ones decorated with a *collarino* in relief. Outstanding among the feminine grave goods were bone objects decorated with circles, bodkins, collars of vitreous paste, mirrors, etc. A chronological pointer is provided by Attic pottery, the superposition of the graves and the discovery of fragments of archaic sculpture in the pavements covering the tumuli.

More than 400 tombs, the oldest belonging to the end of the fifth century B.C., were excavated during 1943 and 1944 in El Cabecico del Tesoro. In 237 B.C. the cemetery was destroyed and re-used; here also ancient sculpture fragments served to support the more recent urns. Attic, Punic and Campanian wares figure on the list of finds as well as native pottery which includes the 'Vase of the Goats', the 'Vase of the Fish' and some terracotta figurines. The vast numbers of falchions,

Plate 58

Plate 62

The Iberians

Fig. 12

'antennae' swords and swords of La Tène II type, as well as four pieces of a belt-plaque showing an eagle above a dove, or possibly a pigeon, are worthy of mention.

Upper Andalusia. The cemeteries in this region are exceptionally large, which relates some of them more closely to the Etruscan tombs than to the megalithic ones previously mentioned. This resemblance is strengthened by the false dome obtained by curved scotias and the pseudo-polygonal or rectangular masonry courses. There would appear to have been a technical leap forward which we cannot directly account for, and which can only be explained by foreign influences.

The most spectacular cemeteries are those of Villaricos (prov. of Almería), Bastia (Baza, prov. of Granada), Tutugi (Galera, of the same province), Tugia (Peal del Becerro, prov. of Jaén), and Tózar, Baena and Almedinilla (all prov. of Córdoba). To these must be added La Guardia (Jaén) and Los Castellones de Ceal (Hinojares, prov. of Jaén) discovered in 1955.

At Villaricos, in the area of mixed colonial and native influences, the following sequence can be established, thanks to the parallel provided by Ceal. There we find a type of cremation within a rectangular grave, like those at Ceal, lying below cremations in urns. At the bottom of these tombs was a rectangular space where the body was burnt; the remains were then gathered and placed in the upper part of the grave above the covering flagstones. The grave goods comprised painted ostrich egg shells, clay lamps of Punic type belonging to the sixth and fifth centuries B.C., rings, scarabs and other articles. The small amphorae with ring-handles, reticulation and a central band are like those of Cruz del Negro and have a Punic origin.

Of the same period are twelve inhumation graves with the skeleton lying in a wooden coffin and having similar grave goods. The masonry tombs complete the ancient part of the cemetery.

The more recent phase of Villaricos is composed of 425 inhumation burials and of cremations with painted pottery in the style of Upper Andalusia and badly classified objects of the period between the fourth and first centuries B.C. The grave goods of the inhumation burials, sometimes of human shape and with wall niches, include ostrich eggs, large amphorae and other objects not later than the second century B.C.

Fig. 39. Limestone cist of Grave 76 at Galera, with traces of painted decoration. Collection of the Marqués de Cerralbo

In the cemetery of Tutugi the 150 tombs were laid out in three zones of which one contained the most massive and also the richest burials. At first it was thought that the other two types of tomb were those of the middle classes and of the humbler inhabitants of the settlement. Later, when smaller graves were discovered within the first area, it was suggested that these might be those of the princes' servants. The burial methods varied greatly. There were urns containing individual cremations which were occasionally placed in rectangular boxes, urns without a cist, cremations without an urn, burials in lime-lined hollows and so on. Close to these simple burials

Plate 15

Fig. 39

κ

lay graves beneath a tumulus with chambers of various shapes. Some, individual or collective, of 'cistern' plan, had their walls strengthened by earth, stones, masonry, flags, beams, etc. Others, of rectangular shape and with a side passage, were sometimes cut in the living rock. There were benches, small walls and partitions within the chambers where lay the urns and offerings. In other burials the grave goods were placed in trenches around the chamber or in inner hollows covered by slabs. Yet another type was of circular plan with a passage under a tumulus and containing a collective cremation. One of these was faced with lime and its lower part was painted red. The oldest burial within this tomb consisted of burnt bones collected in an esparto cloth which was then placed within the urn together with the grave goods.

Another sumptuous tomb has a central column supporting the large roof-blocks. The grave goods took the form of small cists of limestone with painted scenes and various pots, among them some Greek *kraters*. Tomb 82 had some weapons laid on the ground beyond the entrance, and in a hollow in the centre of the chamber lay several Attic bell *kraters* and some weapons. The oldest objects of this cemetery belong to the end of the fifth, and the most recent to the first century B.C.

At Toya (Peal de Becerro) is to be found the biggest grave yet known. It is of trapezoidal plan and divided into three chambers and five compartments, like others, now destroyed, at Almedinilla and Basti. Its door was made up of monoliths supporting a lintel; the central chamber communicated with the aisles and had an interior bench running along the walls with a niche at the end. A tall cornice surmounted the inner side walls, the roof was formed of large stones and the two uppermost blocks of the door-jambs were set at an angle to form a pointed false arch. The left chamber had a vestibule with a rectangular opening in which was fitted a wooden door. At the rear was a bench, and above this a high niche. The

Fig. 40

Fig. 41

Plate 17

Fig. 42

Fig. 40. Section of a Galera grave with painted decoration on its inner wall

147

right-hand chamber possessed an antechamber with benches along two of its walls and a high niche at the rear; on the right-hand wall was another shelf with a stone table supported by a foot-prop against the wall. The tomb was paved with limestone blocks and the walls were of large squared blocks of local limestone, some of them cushioned or cornered and fixed by wedges.

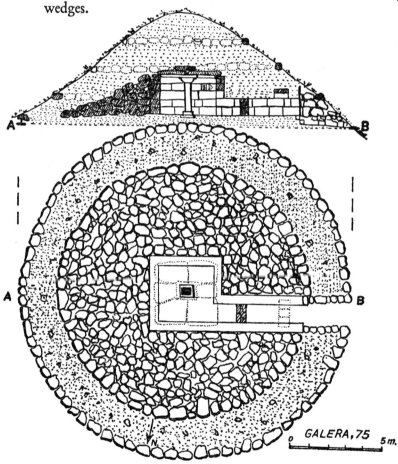

Fig. 41. Plan and section of Grave 75 at Galera

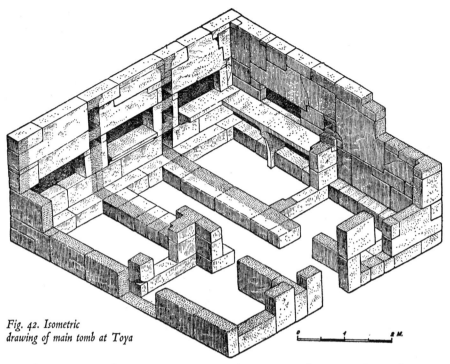

Fig. 42. Isometric drawing of main tomb at Toya

The grave goods are impressive: sculptures, small boxes of painted limestone, weapons, lockets of gilded metal, bronze *situlae*, fibulae, gems and a collection of tools such as socketed sickles and saws. The most spectacular remains, however, are those of a chariot and horse-trappings, such as we associate with princely graves. This tomb presents the most complete architectural achievement known in Iberia; technically it can only be compared with Etruscan architecture.

Beside this tomb were other simple ones consisting of urns above a *bustum* of ashes and with offerings and weapons.

As regards the cemetery of Ceal, we know only the initial excavation results. One grave consisted of a cist covered by a flagstone with four superimposed rows of sun-dried bricks.

Plates 16, 20

Fig. 43

149

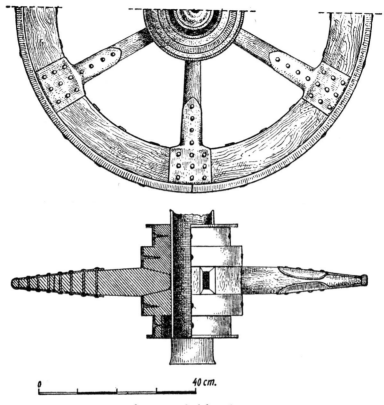

Fig. 43. Reconstruction of a wagon-wheel from the Toya cemetery. Diam. 90 cm.

Another was a rectangular chamber built with sandstone flags covered by sun-dried bricks and stones, with the lower portion of its façade decorated with frescoes of semicircular palmettes. The existence of Celtic graves in a lower level dates the foundation of the settlement to the sixth century B.C.

Four types of graves were found at La Guardia in the same province: *a*) small rectangular tombs of masonry with an inner bench on which were placed the urns and the offerings. These comprised bowls, amphorae, mugs, iron knives, belts with one hook, spindle whorls, a glass *aryballos,* beads of vitreous paste, etc.; *b*) urned cremations within a cavity; *c*) two inhumations in a level above the cremations; *d*) cremations within a cist.

The date of the cemetery is provided by finds of *kylikes* decorated with red figures belonging to the beginning of the fourth century B.C.

Lower Andalusia. The only cemeteries known here are those between Carmona-Mairena and Setefilla (Lora del Rio) in the province of Seville, excavated by George Bonsor. Both cremations and inhumations were found beneath large tumuli, and the grave goods display Celtic and Eastern influences of the sixth or fifth centuries B.C. Perhaps these tumuli are those of orientalized Celts; the only certain fact is that nothing later than the fifth century occurs in these cemeteries. Some of the tumuli yielded Iberian pottery with band-decoration similar to that of Upper Andalusia, suggesting re-use of the tombs.

In Acebuchal there are cremation tumuli where the ashes are covered by fragments of Punic-type amphorae and also other mounds where ritual inhumation in masonry graves prevails. The first type is also found at Alcantarilla, associated with Iberian-Turdetanian pottery, and at Cruz del Negro, the most varied and complicated site of all.

Iberian Art

Fig. 44

F ROM THE PRECEDING CHAPTERS it will have become clear that there was no unifying factor, except the alphabet, in the area lying between Andalusia and the Rhône. This diversity of individual regional centres becomes even more marked when we come to Iberian art.

Sculpture exists only in Andalusia and the Southeast, and sculpture of the human figure does not spread north of Alicante; this fact accounts for the similarity of the work from the different factories and schools of art. Where vase painting, excluding the common element of geometrically decorated pottery, is concerned, we find other local centres of zoomorphic and human decoration. The first occurs only in the Southeast and the second extends throughout the Southeast, the Spanish Levant and the Ebro valley.

Finally, metalwork is restricted to Central and Western Andalusia; the jewellery of these areas is more Tartessian than Iberian in nature.

Bearing all this in mind, let us pass on to another fundamental aspect of Iberian art, namely, its chronology. Lack of proper scientific excavations meant that chronology had to be equated with the study of the evolution of art styles. The evidence of Phoenician and Greek stimuli in Iberian art has suggested that the native form originated from these sources, while the final period was thought to belong to the Roman conquest.

The attribution of the floruit of Iberian art to a period very close to the Roman conquest is in the main due to Professor Garcia Bellido, but this low chronology is open to criticism. He distinguished three periods: 1) Greek provincial, between the fifth and third centuries B.C.; 2) full native development,

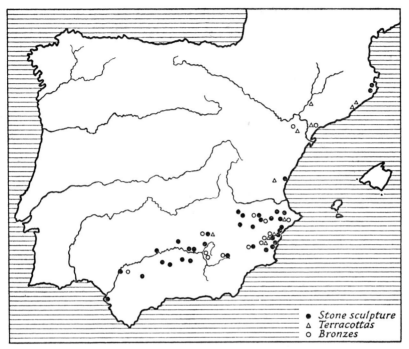

Fig. 44. Finds of stone sculpture of the Iberian period (according to Cuadrado) and distribution of votive offerings of terracotta and bronze

from the end of the third to the first century B.C.; 3) Roman provincial, between the first century B.C. and the fourth century A.D.

The archaic quality of Iberian sculpture is very pronounced. All figures are shown in their frontal aspect; they lack animation and are rigidly conventional. The geometric ornament of the vase-paintings and the very shapes bear this out. But, in 1940, it was impossible to associate the origins of Iberian art with oriental archaism for lack of external evidence. Bellido postulated a pseudo-archaism based on a simple similarity of achievements true to the provincial sculpture of the Western Mediterranean. He was applying the term 'pseudo-archaic' in a chronological sense. But that did not explain the historical and cultural origins of the archaisms of Iberian art. It is no longer possible to fit Iberian art into any absolute geographical or chronological framework. There are forms and patterns in the architectural decoration which derive from Greek and Eastern origins. We can discern some continuity from the Greek Archaic in human and animal statuary both of style and of evolution; some votive offerings also derive from the archaic types found everywhere in the non-classical Mediterranean area.

To accept the classical source of Iberian art is not to deny its originality and its independence, since the classical impact did not efface the historical reality of the native culture. In the past the Iberian area had been assigned to a Mediterranean classical setting, thus endowing it with a formal character which it lacks.

Today the origins of Iberian art can be dated to the fifth century B.C. on the strength of evidence provided by various cemeteries in which fragments of sculpture were re-used in successive phases. Stratigraphical analysis of some settlement sites and cemeteries points to Iberian ceramics having stemmed from Greek and Eastern imports at the close of the sixth century B.C. The forms of Tartessian jewellery also show this identical Greek and Eastern influence at around the same period.

In this manner it is possible to fill the gap that formerly seemed to exist between Archaic Eastern art and the origin of Iberian art. There are still some unsolved problems, for instance the actual means of transmission and the late appearance of scenes of human life in the vase-paintings. The first calls for a serious study of the Mediterranean parallels of native techniques and decoration; the second can be explained as a simple matter of convergence.

In the South and Southeast we find sculptural elements, originally part of monument decoration, among which Eastern prototypes can be distinguished from the products of Iberian background. The majority must be considered as Ionian and Eastern objects, not only by reason of the use to which they were put—capitals, corbels, shafts, lintels and jambs—but also because of the forms taken by their decoration. Ionian and Aeolian volutes, palmettes, friezes of concave or convex *ovoli* and globules found in Andalusia and the Southeast echo the patterns of Syrian and Mycenaean ivories. As opposed to these, native art favoured interlaced patterns conforming more with its taste.

A capital from Elche, decorated with a frieze of palmettes and with its lower volutes enclosed within arcs, offers a typical example of Ionian influence. Its similarity to a capital of the Erechtheum enables us to date it to between 425 and 400 B.C. A newly-found pseudo-Ionian capital from Cadiz and the two Osuna blocks can be assigned to the same art style. In the Osuna relief the collared central column ends in a palmette between two volutes. Its parallels are to be found in a Phoenician capital at Cyprus and in an ivory from Nimrud, both of the sixth century B.C., depicting the 'Tree of Life'.

Plate 24

The bevelled column shaft supporting a corbel in tomb 75 at Tutugi shows the same powerful Ionian-Eastern influence and may be dated to the close of the fifth century B.C.

Fig. 41

Stylistically, the door-jambs of Castulo and El Cigarralejo, with interlaced scrolls, are to be grouped among native products influenced by Ionian-Eastern traditions; that is to say, they are earlier than the fourth century. To these must be added similar finds from Ampurias and Ullastret.

The columns and capitals of Cortijo del Ahorcado at Baeza in Jaén province, decorated with opposed circles within

Plate 25

rectangles, are truly Iberian and belong to the late fourth or the early third century B.C.

ZOOMORPHIC SCULPTURE

The area of zoomorphic sculpture extends from Upper Andalusia to Saguntum in the province of Valencia. The finds at La Guardia (prov. of Jaén) enable us to date a homogeneous group of animal sculptures to the fifth and fourth centuries B.C.

Three stages may be distinguished in the evolution of Iberian zoomorphic sculpture. A first group plainly shows an oriental influence and can be dated to between 550 and 450 B.C. It comprises various monsters, animals or animal-men, the most noteworthy of which are the Beast of Balazote (prov. of Albacete) and the Sphinx of Haches (Bogarra, in the same province). The first has the body of a sitting bull and a man's head, bearded, like that of Achelous; its immediate origin is found in the Greek and Sicilian temples of the sixth century B.C. which have exact replicas of the Balazote Beast. The Sphinx of Haches has a woman's face of wide and triangular outline whose sweetness contrasts with its leer. It must originally have stood with its back against a door, perhaps facing its counterpart.

Plate 10

Plates 8, 9

The Greek provincial series includes the Delphic sphinxes of Agost (prov. of Alicante), the sphinx of Villacarrillo (Jaén) and the griffin of Redován (prov. of Alicante). But the largest group of animals is native and includes lions, wolves, bears, bulls and badly executed sheep. Their immediate origin remains unknown but the distant prototypes are to be found in Syrian and Hittite art. The contracted posture, whether the creature is shown in a sitting or a kneeling position, the open mouth with hanging tongue, the retracted upper lip and other details are traits illustrating a regional aspect of ancient art of Eastern origin.

The appearance of these animals in cemeteries shows that they are linked with the idea of death, and their use as guardians of eternal rest corresponds with the same symbolism as that of the sphinxes. The finding of some fragments of lions *in situ* at the cemetery of La Guardia (prov. of Jaén) proves that they were used as guardian-*stelae* in the fifth and fourth centuries B.C.

Fig. 45. One of the stags from Caudete, Albacete. Limestone, length 75 cm., height 74 cm., thickness 25 cm. Arch. Mus., Albacete

But the recent find of the small golden head of a lion in the River Jándula, in the same province, shows that this style is somewhat earlier as regards jewellery.

Outstanding among all these native series of animals are the lions and lionesses of Baena, Córdoba and Nueva Carteya,

Plate 54

Fig. 45
Plate 53

the bulls of Osuna, Llano de la Consolación, Rojales and Albufereta and the beast of Balones, as well as the recently discovered stags at Caudete. The northern limit of this group is determined by the lionesses of Bocairente and Saguntum in Valencia province. The bulls of the Balearic sanctuary of Costitx can now be linked on artistic grounds with Andalusian animals through the new find at Porcuna.

HUMAN SCULPTURE

Well-executed human sculptures of a distinctive type occur all over the Southeast, while in Osuna (prov. of Seville) is to be found another group uniform in style and chronology.

The stylized hair, eyes and draperies point to an Archaic Greek derivation although the compact stereometric forms (*Blockstil*) hint at Syrian, Hittite and Ionian prototypes. The fact that the main centre was in the densest area of Greek colonization admits no doubt as to its origins.

Plates 12, 13

Some of the sculptures are thought to belong to the school of Greek provincial art, as for instance the fine head of a *kore* (from Alicante?) in Barcelona Museum and the large seated figures from Cabecico del Tesoro, Llano de la Consolación and Cerro de los Santos. The *kore,* wearing a crown of feathers forming a *polos* and a *stephane* without *kestos,* can be related to the type which began with the head of Hera at Olympia. The finest of the seated figures is that from Cabecico del Tesoro; it is

Plate 11
Fig. 46

stiff, draped in a wide robe falling in parallel pleats and seated on an armchair with a tall back. Its most obvious parallels are provided by the seated figures in the temple of Didyma at Miletus (575–550 B.C.). The statue from Llano de la Consolación, likewise very mutilated, is rigid in its posture but its draperies are treated with great freedom.

The native phase of the fifth and fourth centuries B.C. is known by the series of more than 300 sculptures from El Cerro de los Santos. In general these consisted of unattached heads Plate 46 which show a continuous evolution until the Roman period with a pseudo-Archaism to be explained by a late development on the part of the native artists. Between the female head No. 7522 of the National Museum of Madrid, barbarian and

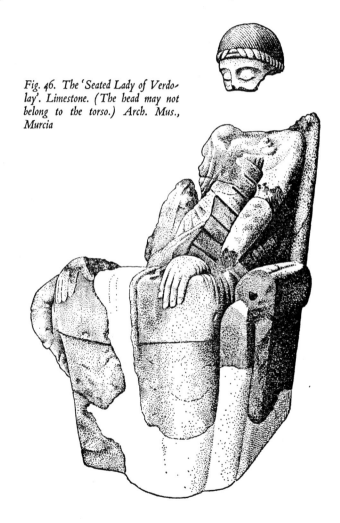

Fig. 46. The 'Seated Lady of Verdo-lay'. Limestone. (The head may not belong to the torso.) Arch. Mus., Murcia

atavistic, and No. 7542 of the same museum, executed by a master hand and perhaps a portrait, lies a wide range of artistry. From this group we should note No. 7510; it is clearly delineated, the fine oval of the face and the eyes following the style found at El Cerro. The 'Cánovas Head' has a curiously archaic aspect.

As regards the male heads, the sculptors have achieved volume and simplicity within an accentuated archaism; occasionally, as in the case of the Barcelona Museum head, an idealistic intuition inspires the artist. It is found also in the male head of El Tolmo de Minateda (prov. of Albacete).

Without a doubt the masterpiece of the native sculptors is the Dama de Elche by reason of her elegant, refined features, the abstract expression of her gaze and the richness of her attire and ornaments. At one and the same time her features are in the Classical tradition, while the representation of her jewels has all the elaboration of the native. This combination is more patent in the Dama, the most important piece of primitive Hispanic art, than in any other product of Iberian art.

The date of the standing priestess known as the Gran Dama of El Cerro has been hotly disputed. Her frontal presentation and profuse decoration, her pleats and her forward-facing feet, as well as her slender cheeks, place her beside the Dama de Elche.

In native sculpture between the third and first centuries B.C., i.e. between the Punic wars and the Christian era, Roman influences become more pronounced, and to them must be added those of the La Tène II period. To this group are allocated some sculptures of the final stage of El Cerro de los Santos, especially the figures wearing togas and the matrimonial groups, as well as the entire series of Osuna reliefs. Particularly fine are the pair of standing votaries carved according to native tradition as regards draperies and features, and those from Tixe in the province of Seville.

Plate 45

Plate 51

Plate 49

Plate 50

Plate 23

Plate 22

Plates 44, 47

Plate 48

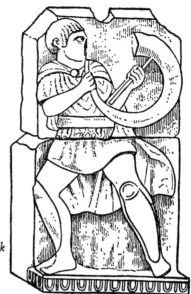

Fig. 47. Horn-player on limestone block from Osuna. Height 1·10 m., width 57 cm., thickness 24 and 16 cm. Nat. Arch. Mus., Madrid

The Osuna reliefs, discovered in 1903, are the best-known Iberian statues. Two of the blocks are worked on two adjacent faces and must have formed part of the corner decoration of the same building. One shows on each side a standing worshipper with regal robes; on the other are seen a beautiful female flute-player and a male figure wearing a cloak. Although the work is very fine, the sculptor lacked a sense of proportion. On another stone two warriors, facing one another on adjacent surfaces, convey a sense of battle by means of a suitable combination of arm and leg movements. Perhaps the most accomplished figure from Osuna is the boy rider occupying the tympanum of a limestone corner-piece; the horse's gallop has been described as 'Velasquez in nature'.

Plate 55

Plate 56

This very homogeneous group must have formed part of the decoration of a building commemorating the events which occurred in Osuna about 50 B.C. at the time of the wars

L

between Caesar and Pompey. Another group from Osuna is of a
later date. It consists of a frieze of warriors grasping swords and
protected by *caetrae*. On another block is depicted a battle
between natives and Romans. A horn-player (*cornicen*) and
an acrobat, both clearly of Roman inspiration, complete the
series of the native Romanized human sculpture found in this
area.

Figs. 15, 16, 20

Plate 57

Figs. 7, 47

SMALL-SCALE SCULPTURE: VOTIVE OFFERINGS

Although the majority of the votive offerings in the sanctuaries
are of bronze there are also some of stone as at El Cigarralejo, and some terracottas as, for instance, at La Serreta de
Alcoy.

Plate 52

The votive offerings in general represent the art and taste of
humble folk; but in some instances, as at El Cigarralejo, the
artists rose above the level of mass production.

The 'master craftsman of El Cigarralejo', in touch with the
best traditions of sandstone and white limestone sculpture of
the Southeastern centres, was inspired by Greek originals and
founded a school whose groups have been classified. It is clear
that he carefully studied the working of muscles and tendons,
and he was at pains to give the impression of movement in his
sculptures and reliefs. The relief depicting a small she-ass with
her little donkey, and two bifacial ones of a mare with her foal
and of two horses, rank among the masterpieces of the Southeast. The little horses and the teams of draught animals from
the sanctuary of La Luz and El Cerro are related to the above,
as are also some reliefs of the 'tamer' of Villaricos.

Plates 35-38

Although the majority of the votive offerings in the Southeast are not later than the second Punic war, the Albufereta
relief is a fine *epigonos* showing a woman weaving in front of a
warrior, a scene whose significance, probably symbolic, escapes
us.

Plate 43

The most important sanctuary as regards plastic art in clay is undoubtedly La Serreta, although votive offerings also occur in lesser number at Castillar and La Luz. More than 300 clay offerings at La Serreta give us an idea of the styles of these female figurines, usually modelled by pinching the clay into shape. Some are related to a pseudo-realistic Eastern art, to the Damas of Ibiza and the sculptures from El Cerro. The group is thought to date from the period of the Roman conquest. Nevertheless in view of the perishable nature of the material, it is quite possible that they were copied from originals of the third century B.C. A fine unpublished composition shows the Mother Goddess suckling twins and surrounded by flute-players; both the technique and the modelling are of great ingenuity. Other small figures are known from Calaceite and Sidamunt.

Plates 39–41

These have appeared in very large quantities in the Andalusian sanctuaries and are difficult to date because they are generally found in refuse dumps and on the surface. They were probably produced in the period between the fourth century and the Roman conquest, but their relation to the buildings and sanctuaries is unknown.

The form they take is very varied; the most numerous are small human figurines, animals, parts of the body, annular fibulae, etc. Some pieces are of good workmanship and were fashioned with chisel and file; others show Classical influence, an unusual occurrence in mass-produced objects.

By far the greatest number are warriors, on foot or on horseback, armed, wearing belted tunics and cloaks. Their attitude is frequently that of votaries or worshippers of the divinity. There are also some naked belted warriors and others of a markedly phallic nature.

The female figurines wear *mitras*, long or short cloaks through which their hands are visible at breast height with outstretched palms bearing doves, fruit and bread in an attitude of offering gifts. Some, like those from La Luz, are naked and of exaggerated corpulence. The belt-buckles, the combs and the ornaments provide chronological links with the larger sculptured figures.

Chapter IX

Pottery

IN ASSESSING the origin and chronology of the Iberian peoples, pottery has proved the crucial factor.

Iberian pots occur with imported wares from the period of Greek vases of the end of the sixth century B.C. down to Roman ware of the first century A.D. At southern Spanish sites we encounter forms and techniques similar to those found in ancient cemeteries of North Africa, for instance the so-called 'red-varnished ware'. Some specimens from the Iberian area are related to others of the Meseta, e.g. the 'Vase of the Dragons' from Hoya de Santa Ana and those with incised collars from El Cigarralejo.

Many problems are raised by local imitations of imported wares. We can now clearly discern imitations of clays, shapes and decoration patterns of Ionic-Phocaean wares in the native settlements close to Massilia, Emporion and Ullastret. Greek forms, for instance *kraters*, were copied in the South of the Peninsula; attempts were also made to imitate Attic black varnish, but these proved unsuccessful and the potters had to be content with the red varnish peculiar to Andalusia. In the same way it seems certain that the black varnishes of Campanian and South Italian wares were also imitated but we have no knowledge either of the kilns or of the native potters.

Another kind of pottery found in conjunction with 'Iberian' wares is the so-called 'Phocaean or Ampurian grey', whose origin, distribution and chronology have not as yet been fully established. In addition to imports there were the common hand-made vessels for domestic use, some of Hallstattian tradition and others of El Argar type which, like the above, occur with 'Iberian' wares.

Fig. 48

Plate 58

Plate 18

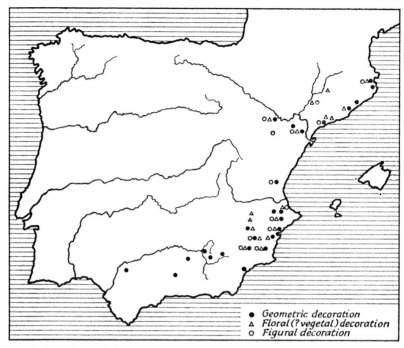

Fig. 48. Distribution of Iberian pottery

Iberian pottery is made of light-coloured clays, yellowish or pink, of porous texture; it is sometimes very thin-walled and always wheel-turned. The shapes of these vessels, with the exception of Greek and Punic imitations, are in many ways peculiar and their evolution is most interesting. They include the *kalathos* or 'goblet', the *oenochoe* with flat base and cylindrical body, the low-footed bowl, the *skyphos* in a native version, and other types. Not all these forms, however, are common to the Iberian area; many are exclusive to a set place or period.

Some pottery kilns used for firing 'Iberian' wares are known: that at Borriól (prov. of Castellón) was of elliptical plan and the smoke escaped through seven chimneys; the one at Rubí (prov. of Barcelona) was square; a grating, supported by a central pillar, separated the baking chamber from the fire below.

The distinguishing feature of Iberian pottery is its painted decoration of iron oxides or manganese which, on backgrounds either smooth or covered with a light slip or a coat of white paint, turned to a wine-red hue. This method of decoration dates back to very ancient times in Mediterranean regions, but the peculiar characteristic of this pottery lies in the wealth and variety of its patterns. These include bands and lines, metopes, concentric semicircles and quarter-circles, lozenges, stylized birds and fishes, plants and even human beings.

Each geographic area adopted its own style of decoration, which was adapted to the special regional shapes; this enables us to differentiate between the various zones of Iberian pottery styles.

Thanks to chronological sequences established in recently excavated sites, we can now assert with confidence that the origin of geometrically decorated Iberian pottery is to be found in Ionic-Phocaean wares in the Northeast of the Peninsula. The date of the native imitations is slightly later than that of the imports; that is, about the end of the sixth or the beginning of the fifth century B.C.

ANDALUSIAN POTTERY WITH GEOMETRIC DECORATION

The appearance in Andalusia of 'geometric' pottery is due to the influence of the Greek colonies in the Southeast (Alonis, Akra Leuké, Hemeroskopeion) as well as to the Phoenician entrepôts of Villaricos and Gades, whose basic patterns are similar with those of Ionia. There is some doubt as to the date when 'geometric' decorated wares appeared in the South, but they are quite likely to have been contemporaneous with the Northeastern imitations, despite regional differences in style and shape.

Fig. 49. Native krater *from Toya imitating Greek* column krater. *These vases average 50 cm. in height. Nat. Arch. Mus., Madrid*

The sequences of El Carambolo and Carmona (prov. of Seville) establish an ornamental tradition of hand-made pottery with reticulated decoration in the sixth century B.C., contemporaneous with the Boquique ('stab and drag') decoration. Above this is found Iberian pottery in conjunction with wheel-turned pots decorated with brown reticulated patterns and 'red varnish' which are dated to the fifth century B.C. The most recent Andalusian Iberian pottery is considered to date to the beginning of our era.

At Ceal (prov. of Jaén) there is, as in Lower Andalusia, a layer of 'stab and drag' pottery above which appear the wares proper to the Phoenician-Tartessian cemeteries. This pottery is coarse, yellowish and monochrome, similar to that of Villaricos dating to around 500 B.C. From then onward occur well-baked urns with red monochrome varnish; these are found together with globular ones having a truncated conical base, which belong to the Celtic tradition.

Plates 16, 19, 20

Fig. 49

At Toya there was a constant imitation of Greek *kraters* and pyxides, decorated with stripes, semicircles and quavers, as well as ovoid, cylindrical and globular urns typical of the general background of other Upper Andalusian sites. These wares do not penetrate into the Meseta region but extend instead into the Southeast (Meca, Minateda, Amarejo and La Bastida de Mogente). Outstanding among the wares of Upper Andalusia are the big ovoid *amphorae* of Tutugi whose shape is of Punic derivation but whose patterns (lozenges, meanders, semicircles and other geometric forms) are Turdetanian.

POTTERY OF THE SOUTHEAST

In the Southeast there exists a whole range of ornamentation which must be considered as the link between the patterns of the South and those of the Spanish Levant. The classical sites of this area are Archena and Elche, to which can now be added El Cigarralejo and Verdolay. Alongside the ancient basic 'geometric' decoration flourished a sober and stylized painting of realistic and floral design accompanied by geometric patterns and stylized creatures such as birds with outspread wings, *carnassiers*, ducks, rabbits and goats. These last forms, more elaborate in detail, spread northwards and occur as far away as Oliva.

The rhythm and elegance of the stylized eagles, as also their sober backgrounds, give this type an outstanding dynamic power and the same applies to the floral geometric decoration. This style reached its peak during the third century B.C. and endured until the Roman conquest.

In this region there existed a school of decoration which used the human figure in two quite different ways. At Elche, the winged Damas placed between horses and the large female heads shown in frontal perspective represents a new approach to symbolism and a new technique; their presence is attested as far north as Ampurias. As opposed to this, human figures appear at Verdolay and Archena in scenes only rivalled by

Plates 67, 68

Plate 61

those of Liria. It is now certain that this school of art began in the third century B.C. and lasted until the first; as a result, the supposed resemblance with East Greek or orientalizing styles must now be totally discarded. The scenes on the 'Vase of the Warriors' from Archena or the battles on the fragments from Verdolay are so skilfully depicted that the realistic and narrative pictures of Liria scarcely bear comparison with them.

POTTERY WITH HUMAN SCENES FROM LIRIA AND THE SPANISH LEVANT

Figs. 3–6, 8–10

The variety of style and subject as well as the great number of well-known scenes make Liria a mine of iconographic information for the understanding of local Iberian life.

One of the predominating techniques at Liria is that of the fully-coloured 'silhouette' displaying a childish and unskilled artlessness. This feature, taken in conjunction with the eccentricity of the backgrounds and the stratigraphical data, leads us to date the *floruit* of this school no earlier than the third century

Fig. 50

B.C. To this group belongs a vase showing a flat-keeled boat in which some men are letting down their nets and casting hooks at fish. Besides this is another scene where riders armed with javelins, shields and bolas are chasing stags.

One of the most moving scenes, because so natural, is that of the hind and her fawn, with which the *stelae* of El Cigarralejo alone are comparable. On the 'Vase of the Ritual Dance' various women in long robes dance hand in hand pursued by an ithyphallic personage. There follows a scene in which a lady offers a dove to a warrior, and finally a battle scene in which a soldier has fallen pierced by a lance. The same technique is used by the artists who decorated the vases known respectively

Fig. 34

as the 'Pomegranate Harvest', the 'Startled Horse' and the 'Two Riders' vases. As opposed to the originators of this cycle another school of art was at work at Liria which specialized in

Fig. 50. Prow of flat-keeled boat (on vase fragment from Liria)

outline figures, paint-filled, with details shown 'in reserve'. There is a sense of spontaneity about this group of varied scenes from life, and the same trait is to be noted in the pictures from La Serreta and Oliva.

Plates 63–66

Filled-in figures of fish, spirals, birds, hearts, etc. provide the accessory decoration, sometimes copied from the Elche-Archena patterns and occasionally accompanied by haphazard alphabetical inscriptions. Sometimes beauty of proportion is attained in the superabundance of decoration, but compositional unity is never achieved.

Human figures are drawn so that the body is seen from the front but the extremities in profile. The artists were unable to resolve the problems of perspective presented by the legs of riders; eyes in profile and horses given a tiptoe gait are merely proof of faulty analytical observation.

The most important achievement of this school are the scenes of the 'Bastetanian Dance'; these constitute a lyrical and delicate presentation of a procession where men and women dance in time to the strains provided by a male and female fluteplayer. Perhaps the scene showing two warriors fighting while two men make music, and that other scene of two horsemen and two foot-soldiers battling serenely to the strains of two trumpets, also represent ritual dances. Another successful composition of this school of art is the 'Frieze of the Warriors', in which a group of men with lances and falchions are fighting others bearing lances and shields; in it we can detect the beginning of that eccentricity which characterizes the ultimate phases of this school.

Fig. 6

One of the most peculiar elements at Liria is provided by the painted ornamental inscriptions which perhaps are explanations of the scenes. This idea can be related to the inscriptions on Attic vases and Greek votive offerings. Since the Lirian alphabet accords with the Roman monetary one, this provides strong supporting evidence for the dating of the vases.

POTTERY FROM THE EBRO VALLEY

Fig. 51

The link between Iberian and Celtic art is to be found in this area. The Azaila pottery is linked with that of the Elche-Archena and the Spanish and Levant through its ivy garlands and the separating of the field of the friezes into 'metopes', and with Celtic symbolism through its bird friezes alternating with

Fig. 51. 'Vase of the Birds' (from Azaila, Teruel)

quadrupeds, human figures and sun-disks. The Azaila fragment depicting a group of men in attitude of the Iberian
salutatio has no connection whatsoever with the Iberian figures   *Fig. 52*
of Liria. 'While the vase-painting of the Elche-Archena school
relied for much of its effect on contrast between straight and
curved outlines, in Azailan vases there is hardly a line that
is not curved: the effect produced is one of rhythm, not of
contrast.'

Something similar can be noted in the human figures from   *Figs. 18, 53–57*
Castellones de Alloza in the province of Teruel. Their style
and the added inscriptions may be ascribed to the Liria 'silhouette' school, but their dynamic quality is Celtic. Briefly,
this area saw the fusion of the concrete and clear-cut Mediterranean mentality with the abstract Celtic character. The

*Fig. 52. Figures in attitude of the Salu-
tatio iberica on small vase from Azaila.
Arch. Mus., Barcelona*

173

Fig. 53. 'Hunter and his dog'; centre-piece of decorated kalathos from Alloza. Arch. Mus., Teruel

links between both artistic traditions are provided by the fragments from Calaceite, in the Lower Aragon, and Sidamunt and Sorba (prov. of Lérida).

CATALONIAN POTTERY

We are now beginning to differentiate between native imitations and Ionic-Phocaean imports; a study of the same phenomenon in Provence (Massilia and La Pègue) and in Languedoc (Cayla and Ensérune) has confirmed the results obtained in Catalonia.

At Ampurias and Ullastret, wares in the Urnfield tradition and Ionian imports of the sixth century B.C. occur in the lower levels. Iberian pottery with bands of ochre on pinkish clays, imitating Ionian wares, is found here as at Cayla and Ensérune prior to 450 B.C.

The Iberian pottery shapes from sites in the Northeast are varied. They include plump urns with sienna slips and red bands, oval urns and, most numerous of all, *kalathoi* with a wealth of ornament (lines, bands, semicircles, quarter-circles, diamonds, quavers, etc.). Sometimes the background is a white slip; this is also occasionally used as decoration. Also of Indicete character are the wares from the middle layers belonging to the fifth and fourth centuries B.C. with slips of reddish-black, sienna, grey and other hues, decorated with continuous

Fig. 58

Fig. 54. Stag-hunt: wolf and birds of prey. Main theme on decorated kalathos *from Alloza. Arch. Mus., Teruel*

Fig. 55. Fragment of decorated kalathos from Alloza. Arch. Mus., Teruel

lines or with dots forming zigzags, meanders and spirals, sometimes in white.

The pottery of Lower Catalonia is different and of a slightly later initial date. On the strength of *graffiti,* discovered at Burriach and Sardanyola (prov. of Barcelona), written in the Iberian alphabet and later than those from Ensérune and Ullastret, we can date its *floruit* in the fourth and third century B.C. The vessel shapes found at Fontscaldes and Sidamunt, mainly taking the form of large *kalathoi* and footed bowls decorated with ivy leaves, recur at Rubí (Barcelona) and other Catalan sites. These wares increased greatly with the Roman conquest, perhaps because they served as containers for exported native products such as honey and salted fish.

Plate 69

The 'Cazurro Vase' from Ampurias constitutes a unique specimen. On it, two hunters wearing a short kilt and coursing stags with javelins are rendered in an impressionistic style. A

Plate 29

Fig. 56. Fragment from same kalathos *as in Fig. 55*

Fig. 57. Fragment from same kalathos *as in Fig. 55*

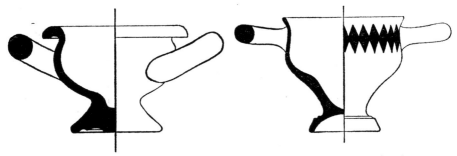

Fig. 58. Two small cups (a) from Cabrera de Mataro. Height 45 mm., rim diam. 60 mm., base diam. 35 mm. (b) with lozenge decoration, from habitation site of Els Castellans. Height 75 mm., rim diam. 80 mm., base diam. 45 mm. Arch. Mus., Barcelona

new element—the landscape—is introduced into the composition in the form of a naturalistically drawn tree. Because of its shape this vase may be considered the prototype of the series whose end-products occur at Elche, Liria and Calaceite, and can be dated to the fifth century B.C.

CHAPTER X

Tartessian-Iberian Jewellery

T HE RECOGNITION of a native style and technique in the art of metalworking is the latest addition to our knowledge of Iberian archaeology. Although a large percentage of the patterns and forms of pre-Roman jewellery are in the Oriental tradition, their style of rendering and the use of altered techniques bear the Iberian impress. Today it seems certain that Tartessian-Iberian jewellery represents a special Mediterranean province in the same way as does Etruscan art.

The skill of the jewellers and metalworkers of the South lay in the way they combined Eastern and Celtic influences; the resulting synthesis was both personal and daring.

We may conveniently divide this chapter into three sections, dealing with Tartessian jewellery, Andalusian jewellery, and that of a marginal Spanish Levantine area, respectively. The first category includes styles showing oriental influence; this jewellery was made from the sixth to the fifth century B.C. The manufacture of Andalusian (or Turdetanian) jewellery was begun between the fifth and fourth centuries B.C. and continued until the Roman period; it illustrates Celtic contributions to the oriental tradition.

Fig. 59

TARTESSIAN JEWELLERY

The Tartessian area has produced the richest and largest series of finds in the Peninsula. Lack of external evidence obliges us to date these objects entirely by style-classification.

The treasure of La Aliseda (prov. of Cáceres) includes earrings, bracelets, necklaces, small chains, appliqué-work, eardrops, rings, seals and other more important objects. One of these is the golden belt which, on a granulated background,

Plate 2

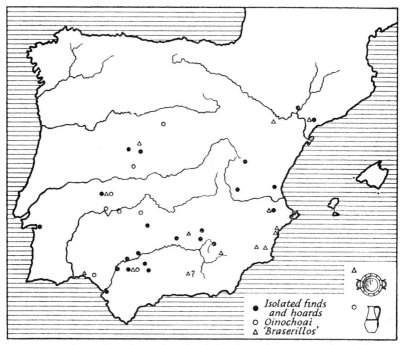

Fig. 59. Distribution of jewellery and metalwork (sixth–second centuries B.C.), and of 'braserillos' and oenochoai

bears a lion-tamer, a griffin and palmettes. Its Eastern and Phoenician prototypes are readily recognizable although the same patterns also appear in the Regolini-Galassi tomb of Etruria, of identical inspiration but of different technique. Some palmettes are the same as those of the Carmona ivories (some of them now assumed to be native productions) and those of the Galera paintings.

Plate 5

Plate 1

Plate 3

The diadem, despite its remote Eastern origin, denotes an Etruscan influence and a Tartessian background, as do also the ear-rings with oriental motifs of hawks and palmettes interpreted in a Western manner. The bracelets and the necklace comprise various elements, such as amulets with capsules, similar to all the products of Western art with Eastern trends. The seal showing the 'tree of life' between rampant griffins beneath palmettes, with the Egyptian hawk as crown and having a divinity on either side, may well be a Syrian import although its connexions seem closest with Cyprus (600–475 B.C.) and Vulci.

This area to the North of the Guadiana illustrates the extent to which the centres in the Guadalquivir region spread. A scarab of Psammeticus the First, related to the Aliseda imports, is known from Alcacer do Sal in Portugal. To the same area and background belong various bronze *oenochoai* (some of them with stags' heads) which have parallels in the Guadalquivir region. They are nowadays dated to the sixth century B.C. and their centre of origin is reckoned to be either Gades or Tartessos. These flagons, together with the bronze *braserillos*, constituted a ritual 'set' whose distribution area extended from La Aliseda to Tivissa, i.e. from the west to Catalonia. The

Fig. 60

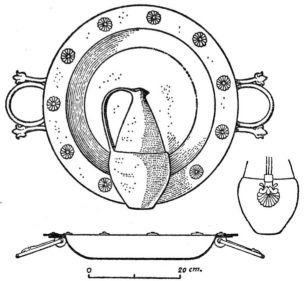

Fig. 60. 'Braserillo' and flagon of bronze. From the tumulus of La Canada de Ruiz Sanchez, Carmona (prov. Seville)

Tartessian group is older, being dated to the sixth century B.C.; whereas that of Upper Andalusia and the Southeast (Galera and Cigarralejo) belongs to the fourth. They then became known to the Celts of the Meseta, who in their turn transmitted them to the Iberians of the Spanish Levant between the fourth and the second centuries B.C.

Plate 6

The most recent and sensational find of jewellery is that of El Carambolo, near Seville. It comprises 21 items of 24-carat gold and has a total weight of 2,950 grammes. Each item consists of two strips soldered peripherally, smoothed or plainly scored within and having protuberant and sunken zones without. The greater part of the decoration is soldered on to the plates. One group of these objects is ornamented with rosettes and hemispheres, another with scales, hoops and hemispheres with a sunken centre.

The first of these groups includes a breastplate, two twin cylindrical bracelets and eight rectangular plaques. The breastplate is shaped like an ox-hide ingot and has a framework of four tubular pieces through which were threaded suspension strings. Its decoration takes the form of rows of hemispheres and stamped rosettes mounted in capsules within a border of indented and raised fillets of smaller size. Each bracelet is composed of two superimposed cylindrical plates decorated in the same fashion as the breastplate. A series of eight plaques (four

Plate 7

smaller ones decorated with three rows of rosettes and four larger ones with four rows of rosette-like ornament) are also pierced for suspension.

The second group comprises another breastplate, eight rectangular plaques and a necklace. The breastplate has rows of

Fig. 61

hemispheres alternating with rows of flat rings along the border. There is a central vertical strip overlaid with hollowed hemispheres and surrounded by circles and flat scales. The plaques have the same decoration as those described above but this is executed in the technique of scales or imbricated arcs.

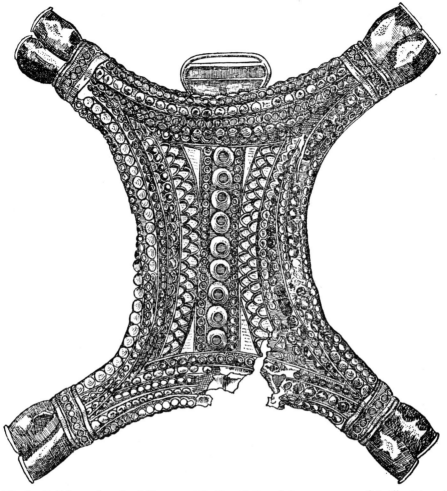

Fig. 61. Gold breast-plate shaped like an ox-hide. Part of Carambolo treasure, prov. of Seville. Diagonal width 170 mm. Arch. Mus., Seville

The necklace has seven pendants of signet rings whose hoops and seals are adorned in a peculiar manner. This ornamentation consists of parallel bars, disks and scales on the screens closing the ring's inner portion, as well as zones of triangles on the capsules' walls. The oval and flat surfaces of

Fig. 62

the seals carry floral patterns, some very Eastern-looking and others of Archena type, on a background of hemispheres arranged in rows.

The plaques were worn joined together as a crown, in the same manner as the Phoenician-Cypriot example in the Schiller collection. Those with smooth hemispheres have parallels in the archaic pendants of Thessaly, while their successors are the ones from Santiago de la Espada and the drum-shaped disks of the Dama de Elche.

The necklace can be compared with examples from Aliseda and with others from Etruria and the East at the start of the sixth century B.C. Although the rosettes are Eastern in conception, their conjunction with capsules is unknown outside Iberia. The scales are somewhat similar to those of the ivory thrones of Samos and Nimrud and some Proto-Corinthian vases but they have no parallels in jewellery.

There is a fusion of skill and of style both delicate and barbaric in this collection of jewellery, and a combination of Eastern and native influences. It is of high technical quality but shows little imagination in its patterns. It can be dated to the early part of the sixth century B.C. and is somewhat later in style than the Aliseda hoard.

Fig. 63

Yet another treasure was found at the Evora farmstead near Sanlúcar de Barrameda in the province of Cadiz. It includes a diadem with granulated work like that at Aliseda and Jávea, eight portions of a bracelet showing similarities to jewels from Rhodes and Tharros, as well as some sheaths and beads with the same decoration (a stylized human figure); the prototypes of the latter are Egyptian-Cypriot cartouches, which also inspired the artist of Aliseda. Two ear-rings with pendants and

Fig. 64

part of a necklace decorated with rosettes, buds, disks and crescents belong to the same tradition.

This type of necklace with capsules is also found at La Cruz del Negro (prov. of Seville) and, at a later date, on the Dama de

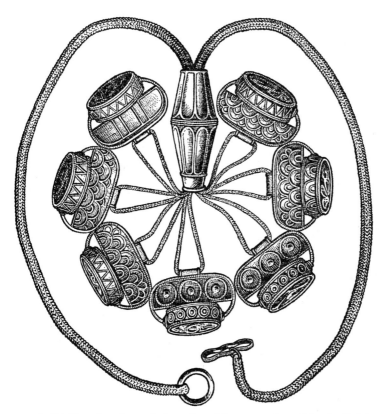

Fig. 62. Necklace of pendant seals from Carambolo treasure. Overall length of chain 600 mm. Arch. Mus., Seville

Elche. The Tartessian finds ultimately derive from an ancient Eastern source which can also be traced in the figures from the sanctuaries of Tanit-Demeter in Ibiza and Sicily; there may be a link, too, with the hypothetical Rhodian journeys.

In Upper Andalusia a good example of Tartessian workmanship is provided by a small golden head of a lion from the River Jándula (prov. of Jaén) which can be paralleled with Rhodian jewellery of the seventh century B.C.

Fig. 63. Gold necklace-pendant, with granulations depicting human figure. Height 26 mm. From Cortijo de Evora, prov. of Cadiz. Arch. Mus., Cadiz

Fig. 64. Gold ear-pendant from Cortijo de Evora, prov. of Cadiz. Length 24 mm., max. width 24 mm. Arch. Mus., Cadiz

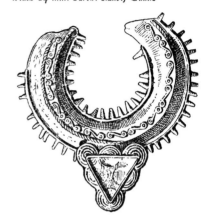

The brisk spread of Tartessian jewellery and metalwork could well account for finds of jewels of this style in regions of the Meseta. Such are, for instance, the portion of a griffin-decorated belt from Sanchorreja (prov. of Avila) which has parallels at Aliseda and Carmona and the goddess from Cerro del Berrueco in the province of Salamanca.

ANDALUSIAN JEWELLERY OF THE FIFTH CENTURY B.C.

Plate 60

From the fifth century B.C., Upper Andalusia seems to have come into contact with Celtic influences. Celtic niello and repoussé work, especially on brooches, belt-buckles and falchions, replaces Tartessian techniques and patterns, and overlaps with them and with those of Eastern tradition—such as granulation and filigree. We see this mingling of styles in small hoard finds; their objects show Tartessian inspiration, Celtic influences and Greek and even Hellenistic tendencies. An instance is provided by the treasure of Abengibre (prov. of Córdoba), whose silver vases with Iberian markings and chased palmettes and rosettes date from the fourth century B.C. The same applies to the hoard of Molino de Marrubial (Córdoba), which was several centuries old when buried in 104 B.C. That of Los Almadenes de Pozoblanco, also in Córdoba province, is composed of heterogeneous objects of which the most noteworthy are silver fibulae adorned with the foreparts of conjoined horses, with lizards, dogs, horses and wild boars which are Celtic in technique and decoration.

Plate 59

The hoard of Mogón (prov. of Jaén) is by far the most complete in every sense and the latest of its coins, which belong to the Roman consulate of the year 89 B.C., tells us when it was buried. It includes silver torques, armlets and bracelets, a Hellenistic medallion and other valuable objects. Among these the most important are the sheath plate of a dagger with animal figures set in a border, a diadem decorated with scrolls, rosettes and birds between wavy lines and, notably, a buckle formed by a duck joined to a half-moon and ornamented with rows of circles, dog's-tooth patterns, waves and leaves. This extremely diverse collection displays a strong Hellenistic influence despite the fact that some of the objects, such as the torques, have Tartessian and Celtic antecedents.

Plates 75-77

A jeweller's hoard was found at Santiago de la Espada. It included ingots, fragments of vases, and crucible cakes (all destined for the melting-pot), contained in a silver vase of Celtic shape whose cover was a silver *patera* decorated with an eccentric star (engraved and gilded) and having an Iberian inscription similar to that of Abengibre. Besides objects of Celtic inspiration, there are some ear-rings with granulated clusters and another pair with twin-winged Damas. These are Tartessian in conception and their technique of granulation

Plate 4 and soldering recalls that of El Carambolo. The figures rest on small pillars, and the granulation and the workmanship of the helmets, the rosettes and the ribbons are outstanding and related to pottery patterns of the Southeast. The globules with reserved crosses among granulation represent one of the most brilliant technical achievements of Tartessian-inspired jewellery in the third century B.C.

The finds of Juan Abad (prov. of Ciudad Real) and Salvacañete (prov. of Cuenca) carry the trail of treasure-hoards up to the Meseta; they illustrate the mingling of influences in these regions of contact.

JEWELLERY FROM THE SPANISH LEVANTINE-CATALAN REGION

The Mediterranean coastal area has provided some isolated objects showing a powerful Greek influence acting upon Iberian techniques and patterns. Such, for instance, is the Jàvea diadem
Plate 79 on which Greek subjects of Eastern origin are treated in a special way; namely, in parallel zones of friezes and in patterns inspired by pottery of the Southeast.

This unusual object apart, the bracelets and small chains of Jávea belong to the third century B.C. as do the other finds of this area; namely, the chain from Bastida de les Alcuses and the silver torques, fibulae and bracelets of Cheste.

Native jewellery in the Ebro region is illustrated by the
Tivissa finds which include *phialai* with gilded spirals, fish, etc., as well as the *phiale* decorated with religious scenes referred to above. A collection of silver vases is linked by their shape with those of the South used for offerings. To these must be added the ear-rings, some with cupids and others with granulated clusters of spirals, undoubtedly in the Andalusian tradition.
Plate 78 The necklace from la Valleta del Valeroso (Serós, prov. of Lérida) with a hammered and chiselled lion's head, very poorly

executed, may be dated to the second century B.C.; that is to say, to the final period, when Andalusian jewellery was imitating the Hellenistic style.

Such are the complexities of Tartessian-Iberian jewellery and metalwork, a craft in which so many elements became merged in the course of centuries. Eventually these ended in the destruction of that ancient and powerful Andalusian centre whose wealth of themes and technical brilliance had flourished in such splendour.

At the present time the possibility of attributing the Carmona ivories to native craftsmen is being discussed. Technical details, such as the incised designs which are unlike the relief-work of Eastern ivories, appear to support the case for native provenance.

Appendix

The sources of ancient Hispania have been collected, edited, translated and annotated in *Fontes Hispaniae Antiquae* (F.H.A.), University of Barcelona. So far the following volumes have appeared in Spanish:

I. *Avienus. Ora Maritima*, ed. Schulten. Barcelona 1922.
II. *From 500 B.C. to Caesar.* ed. Schulten. Barcelona 1925.
III. *The wars between 237 and 154 B.C.*, ed. Schulten. Barcelona 1935.
IV. *The wars between 154 and 72 B.C.*, ed. Schulten. Barcelona 1937.
V. *The wars between 72 and 19 B.C.*, ed. Schulten (with notes). Barcelona 1940.
VI. *Strabo. Geography of Iberia*, ed., trans. and annot. Schulten. Barcelona 1952.
VIII. *The Sources, from Caesar to the fifth century A.D.*, ed. and annot. R. Grosse. Barcelona 1959.

Avienus has also been edited and annotated by BERTHELOT: *Festus Avienus. Ora Maritima.* Paris 1933.

Compare the critique of Schulten by CLERC: F.H.A. vol. I, in *Massilia* II, p. 159. Strabo's *Geography* has also been published and annotated by A. GARCIA BELLIDO: *España y los españoles hace 2000 años según la Geografía de Strábón.* Madrid 1945.

Vol. VII of the F.H.A. which deals with Mela and Pliny has not yet appeared but editions of these writers on the subject of Iberia are available in A. GARCIA BELLIDO's *La España del siglo I de nuestra Era según P. Mela y C. Plinio.* Madrid 1947.

Texts prior to 500 B.C. refer to Western myths and to Tartessos and its legendary kings. There are Assyrian and biblical allusions to Tarshish; the Hesperides, the Ocean, Geryon and the island of Erythia are discussed by Hesiod (*Theogony*) and Stesichoros (apud Strabo 1,148). Hecateus (500 B.C.) is quoted by Stephanos of Byzantium as mentioning various peoples and cities of the Peninsula.

The most interesting source is the *Periplus* of Avienus, the *Ora Maritima*, written in late Roman times, whose Book I has come down to us. It describes the journey by ship from Tartessos to Massilia and makes use of a Massiliot *Periplus* of the sixth century B.C. with added reports on the Ocean's coasts between Tartessos and the Oestrymnides. Avienus used this earlier *Periplus* thanks to an adaptation by Ephorus (fourth century B.C.) and a compilation of Scymnos (first century B.C.). The numerous interpolations make a critique of the text extremely arduous and, as a result, the exponents of Avienus are divided into two groups. The first holds that his work contains sources of the sixth century B.C. whereas the second believes that the earliest sources belong to the fourth century of that era.

There are references to Iberia dating back to the fifth century B.C. These include Himilco's *Periplus* of about 500 B.C. (in Pliny, *Nat. Hist. 2*, 169); that of Hanno concerning the Columns of Hercules; Pindar, who tells us that the Straits were then closed to ships; and Aeschylus who refers to the Erydanus and the Gorgons of the West.

Towards the middle of the fifth century B.C., Herodotus refers to tribes dwelling near the Straits as Iberians and names as such the Kinetes, Celtes, Tartessians, Elbysinians, Mastienians and Kelkianians. He also mentions the Iberian mercenaries in Magna Graecia and Sparta, the Phocaean journeys to Tartessos, Colaius of Samos, the peoples of the Northwest, the Erydanus and the esparto and ferrets of Iberia.

Between 440 and 380 B.C. the authorities are Antiochus of Syracuse (in Diodorus) who held that the Sicani were natives of Sicily; Hellanicus of Lesbos, who, like Thucydides, believed them to have come from Iberia; Herodorus of Heraklea, who names the tribes of the Straits from West (the Kinetes) to East (the Mastienians); and Aristophanes who, like Diodorus, discusses Iberian mercenaries in Sicily.

Ephorus (405–340), using earlier sources and himself later quoted by Strabo, Stephanos of Byzantium and Scymnos, distinguishes the Tartessians from the Iberians, mentions the existence of Emporion, the arrival of the Celts at Gades, the presence of tin in the river of Tartessos and the occupation of the south coast by the Ethiopians. Scylax of Cariadna (*c.* 340), who describes Gades and its situation, the terrors of the Ocean and his seven-day journey from the Straits to Emporion, has much in common with Ephorus. According to Scylax the Iberians on occasions reached the Rhône.

Around 330 Pytheas of Massilia defied the blockade in the Straits and ventured through the Ocean as far as the Oestrymnides, thus rediscovering the peninsular nature of Iberia. Pytheas is the source used by Eratosthenes on the subject of the Ocean; his descriptions are contradicted by those of Artemidorus and Polybius.

Timaeus (340–250) collects the reports of Ephorus about Iberia and those of Pytheas concerning the Ocean; he also describes the Balearics and their inhabitants.

After 200 B.C. we are fairly well informed about Iberia thanks to Polybius, Artemidorus, Posidonius, Asclepiades and Strabo. Polybius was present, with Scipio, at the destruction of Numantia in 133 B.C. and travelled throughout the Peninsula as well as making use of the reports of the Roman generals. His work represents a great step forward in ethnography but a retrogressive one regarding the geography of the Peninsula. His very fragmentary descriptions recur in Strabo and Appian who uses them especially when writing about the Celtiberian and Lusitanian wars.

The *Geographoumena* of Artemidorus (*c.* 100 B.C.) deals with the coastal regions and the customs of the inhabitants. His Book II (lost like the rest) was frequently followed by Strabo and Stephanos of Byzantium. He places some of the Iberian peoples, denies the existence of Tartessos and mentions the Greek centres of the Southeast. His references to the Ocean's tides at Gades are interesting from a geographic viewpoint; and so, from an ethnographic aspect, is also his knowledge of the coastal sanctuaries.

Posidonius (130–60 B.C.) discusses the Peninsula in his introduction to the Lusitanian and Celtiberian wars. He journeyed through Hispania and studied the coastal region between Massilia and Gades. He reserves the name of Iberia for the eastern portion of the Peninsula and is admirably well-informed regarding Turdetania. He writes of battles, clothes, weapons, food, mines, hydrography and so forth, and even collects ancient myths. Asclepiades of Mirlea, a master of rhetoric in Hispania, follows Posidonius and Artemidorus and so does Strabo (65 B.C.–A.D. 20). Although the last had no personal knowledge of the Peninsula, he made excellent use of earlier sources and his treatment of Iberian geography as a whole is extremely interesting.

The *Orbis Pictus*, a mural map painted by Agrippa's orders on his daughter's (Vipsania Polla) portico, and the *Chorographia* explaining it, influenced two writers on Iberian affairs—Pomponius Mela and Pliny the Elder. In Mela's Handbook and in Pliny's Encyclopedia of Sciences are to be found many varied and interesting items concerning Iberia.

A century later Ptolemy, in his *Geography*, lists and names Hispanic localities and gives their geographical position with mathematical precision. The place-names and the administrative tribal boundaries of the land are most helpful in our knowledge of the earlier phases.

Livy is also useful when he employs trustworthy sources but he is apt, on occasions, to accept all sorts of strange reports.

Bibliography

Abbreviations

A.E.A.Arq.	*Archivo Español de Arte y Arqueología.* (*Madrid. C.S.I.C.*)
A.E.Arq.	*Archivo Español de Arqueología.* (*Madrid. C.S.I.C.*)
A.P.L.	*Archivo de Prehistoria Levantina.* (*Valencia*)
An. Hist. A.M.	*Anales de Historia Antigua y Media de la Facultad de Filosofía y Letras de la Universidad de Buenos Aires.*
B.S.E.	*Boletín del Seminario de Estudios de Arte y Arqueología de la Universidad de Valladolid.*
C.A.S.E.	*Congresos Arqueológicos del Sudeste.*
C.C.P.P.	*Congreso Internacional de Ciencias Prehistóricas y Protohistóricas. IV. Madrid, 1954.* (*Zaragoza 1956*)
C.F.A.	*Cuerpo Facultativo de Archiveros, Bibliotecarios y Arqueólogos.* (*Madrid*)
C.G.E.A.	*Comisaría General de Excavaciones Arqueológicas.* (*Madrid*)
C.H.P.	*Cuadernos de Historia Primitiva.* (*Madrid*)
C.I.L.	*Corpus Inscriptionum Latinorum.*
C.N.A.	*Congresos Nacionales de Arqueología.*
C.S.I.C.	*Consejo Superior de Investigaciones Científicas.* (*Madrid*)
C.V.H.	*Corpus Vasorum Hispanorum.*
Emerita	*Boletín de Linguistica y de Filología Clásica.* (*Madrid*)
I.E.C.	*Institut d'Estudis Catalans.* (*Barcelona*)
I.E.G.	*Instituto de Estudios Gerundenses.* (*Gerona*)
I.L.N.	*Illustrated London News.*
J.S.E.A.	*Memorias de la Junta Superior de Excavaciones.* (*Madrid*)
M.P.E.	*Menéndez Pidal, R. Estudios dedicados a Ménendez Pidal.* (*Madrid*)
M.P.H.	*Menéndez Pidal, R., editor. Historia de España.* (*Madrid*)
P.P.S.	*Proceedings of the Prehistoric Society.* (*Cambridge*)
Rev. Arch. Bibl. Mus.	*Revista de Archivos, Bibliotecas y Museos.* (*Madrid*)

Rev. Id. Estét.	*Revista de Ideas Estéticas.* (*Madrid*)
S.P.P.	*Symposium de Prehistoria de la Península Ibérica, 1.* (*Pamplona 1959*)
Saitabi	*Saitabi. Universidad de Valencia.*
Sefarad	*Sefarad. Revista de Estudios Hebraicos y Oriente Próximo.* (*Madrid-Barcelona*)
Zephyrus	*Zephyrus. Revista de la Universidad de Salamanca.*

CHAPTER I *Identifying the Iberians*

P. BOSCH GIMPERA: *Etnologia de la Península Ibérica.* Barcelona 1932.

J. CAMON: *Las artes y los pueblos de la España primitiva.* Madrid 1954.

J. CARO: *Los pueblos de España.* Barcelona 1946.

P. DIXON: *The Iberians of Spain.* Oxford 1940.

J. MALUQUER: Pueblos Ibéricos. *M.P.H.* I, 3. 1954.

J. MARTINEZ SANTAOLALLA: *Esquema paletnologico de la Península Ibérica.* Madrid 1941.

O. MENGHIN: Migrationes Mediterraneae. Origen de las ligures, iberos aquitanos y vascos. *Runa* I (Buenos Aires 1948), p. 111.

L. PERICOT: España Antigua. in *Hist. de España.* Barcelona 2nd ed. 1958.

L. PERICOT: *La España primitiva.* Barcelona 1950.

A. SCHULTEN: *Numantia.* I. Munich 1914.

The Iberian problem is discussed in the following papers: *S.P.P.* pp. 195–219; 221–256; 273–300.

CHAPTER II *The Land*

P. DEFFONTAINES and M. DURLIAT: *España del Levante* (*Cataluña, Baleares y Valencia*). Barcelona 1958. (Translated from the French)

E. HERNANDEZ PACHECO: *Fisiografía del solar hispano.* Madrid 1956.

J. KLEIN: *La Meseta; estudio de la historia económica española.* Madrid 1936. (Translated from the German)

A. SCHULTEN: *Iberische Landeskunde. Geographie des Antiken Spanien.* I. Strasbourg 1955.

J. SERMET: *L'Espagne du Sud.* Paris 1953.

I. SOLE SABARIS: *España. Geografía física.* Barcelona, I, 1952; II, 1954.

N*

CHAPTER III *Formation of the Iberian Peoples*

A. ARRIBAS: Megalitismo peninsular. *S.P.P.* pp. 69–102.

A. BELTRAN: La indoeuropeización del valle del Ebro. *S.P.P.* pp. 103–124.

P. BOSCH GIMPERA: *El poblamiento antiguo y la formacion de los pueblos de España.* Mexico 1944.

R. LANTIER: Celtas e iberos. Contribución al estudio de sus culturas. *A.E.Arq.* XIV (1940–1941) pp. 141–181.

J. MALUQUER: El proceso histórico de las primitivas poblaciones peninsulares. II. *Zephyrus.* VI (1955) pp. 241–255.

M. TARRADELL: Problemas del Neolitico. *S.P.P.* pp. 45–68.

Greeks, Phoenicians and Carthaginians:

A. GARCIA BELLIDO: *Hallazgos griegos en España.* Madrid 1936.

A. GARCIA BELLIDO: *Hispania Graeca.* Barcelona 1948.

A. GARCIA BELLIDO: Nuevos hallazgos griegos en España. *A.E.Arq.* XIV (1940–1941) pp. 524–538.

A. GARCIA BELLIDO: *Fenicios y carthagineses en Occidente.* Madrid 1942.

M. TARRADELL: El impacto colonial de los pueblos semitas. *S.P.P.* pp. 257–272.

Romanisation:

A. BALIL: Un factor difusor de la romanización: las tropas hispanicas al servicio de Roma (III–I cent. B.C.). *Emerita.* XXIV (1956) pp. 108–135.

A. BALIL: Algunos aspectos del proceso de la romanización en Cataluña. *Ampurias.* XVII–XVIII (1955–1956) pp. 39–57.

P. PALOL: Etapas de la romanización. *S.P.P.* pp. 303–317.

C. SANCHEZ ALBORNOZ: Proceso de la romanización de España desde los Escipiones hasta Augusto. *An. Hist. A.M.* (1949).

J. de C. SERRA RAFOLS: El poblamiento romano de Hispania. *C.C.P.P.* pp. 911–929.

Tartessos:

M. ALMAGRO: El hallazgo de la Ria de Huelva y el final de la Edad del Bronce en el occidente europeo. *Ampurias*. II (1940) pp. 85–143.

M. ALMAGRO: *Inventaria Archaeologica*. E.1. Madrid 1958.

C. HAWKES: Las relaciones en el Bronce final entre la Península Ibérica y las Islas Británicas. *Ampurias*. (1952) pp. 81–121.

H. HENCKEN: The fibula of Huelva. *P.P.S.* (1956) pp. 213–215.

H. HENCKEN: Carp's tongue swords in Spain, France and Italy. *Zephyrus*. VII (1956) pp. 125–178.

E. MACWHITE: *Estudios sobre las relaciones atlánticas de la Peninsula Hispánica en la Edad del Bronce*. Madrid 1951.

J. MALUQUER: Nuevas orientaciones en el problema de Tartessos. *S.P.P.* pp. 273–301.

H. N. SAVORY: The Atlantic Bronze Age in South West Europe. *P.P.S.* 1949 p. 128.

A. SCHULTEN: *Tartessos*. 2nd ed. Madrid 1945.

CHAPTER IV *The People*

J. and M. E. CABRE: La caetra y el scutum en Hispania durante la segunda Edad del Hierro. *B.S.E.* VI (1939–1940) pp. 57–84.

J. CARO: La escritura en la España Prerromana (Epigrafía y Numismática). *M.P.H.* I, 3 (1954) pp. 677–812.

A. GARCIA BELLIDO: Música, danza y literatura entre los pueblos primitivos de España. *Rev. Id. Estét.* (1943) p. 59.

A. GARCIA BELLIDO: *Bandas y guerrillas en las luchas con Roma*. Madrid 1945.

J. GIMENO: La indumentaria del jinete ibérico. *Cat. Exp. Numis.* Tarrasa 1951.

M. GOMEZ MORENO: La escritura bástulo-turdetana (primitiva hispánica). *Rev. Arch. Bibl. Mus.* LXIX, 2, 1961, pp. 879–948.

H. HENCKEN: Indo-European languages and archaeology. *Amer. Anthr. Assoc.* 57, no. 6 pt. 3, 1955.

H. SANDARS: The weapons of the Iberians. *Archaeologia*. LXIV (1913) pp. 1–105.

A. TOVAR: *The Ancient languages of Spain and Portugal*. New York 1961.

A. TOVAR: Léxico de las inscripciones ibéricas (celtibérico e ibérico). *M.P.E.* II. (1951) pp. 273–323.

A. TOVAR: Sobre las escrituras tartessia, libio-fenicia y del Algarbe. *Zephyrus.* VI (1955) pp. 273–283.

R. VIOLANT: Un arado y otros apero ibéricos hallados en Valencia. *Zephyrus.* IV (1953) pp. 119–130.

CHAPTER V *Habitation Sites and Houses*

M. ALMAGRO: Estratigrafía de la ciudad helenistico-romana de Ampurias. *A.E.Arq.* XX (1947) pp. 179–199.

I. BALLESTER and others: *Cerámica del Cerro de San Miguel de Liria. C.V.H.* Madrid 1954.

H. BREUIL and R. LANTIER: Le Tolmo a Minateda. *A.P.L.* II (1945) pp. 213–237.

A. DEL CASTILLO: La Costa Brava en la Antiguedad. *Ampurias* I (1939) pp. 186–267.

A. GARCIA BELLIDO: *La arquitectura entre los iberos.* Madrid 1945.

M. OLIVA: Sobre las excavaciones en Ullastret. *A.I.E.G.* VIII (1953) pp. 296–316; IX (1954) pp. 272–316; X (1955) pp. 322–410; XI (1956–1957) pp. 274–338; XII (1958) pp. 319–337; XIII (1959).

A. SCHULTEN: Meca, una cuidad rupestre ibérica. *C.A.S.E.* Albacete (1946) pp. 265–279.

J. de C. SERRA RAFOLS: Llocs d'habitació iberics de la Costa de Llevant. *A.I.E.C.* (1927–1931) pp. 41–54.

S. VILASECA and others: Excavaciones del Plan Nacional en el Castellet de Bañolas de Tivisa (Tarragona). *C.G.E.A.* 20 (1949).

CHAPTER VI *Social Life, Trade and Economy*
Economics:

J. CARO: Regímenes sociales y políticos de la España pre-romana. *Rev. Id. Estét.* I–II. Madrid 1940.

A. GARCIA BELLIDO: *España y los españoles hace dos mil años.* Madrid 1945.

G. Gosse: Las minas y el arte minero de España en la Antigüedad. *Ampurias.* IV (1942) pp. 43–68.

J. Jauregui and E. Poblet: Minería antigua en cabo de Palos. *C.A.S.E.* III (Murcia, 1947) pp. 79–97.

J. de C. Serra Rafols: Els començos de la mineria; metallurgia del coure a la península Ibérica. *Bul. de L'Assoc. Cat. de Ant. Etnol. Prehist.* 1924.

Coins:

J. Amoros: *Les dracmes emporitanes.* Barcelona 1933.

J. Amoros: *Les monedes emporitanes anteriors a les dracmes.* Barcelona 1934.

A. Beltran: *Numismática antigua.* Cartagena 1950.

M. Grant: The decline and fall of city coinage in Spain. *Numis. Chron.* IX (1949).

Guadan: *Las leyendas ibéricas en las dracmas de imitación emporitana.* Madrid 1956.

G. F. Hill: *Notes on the ancient coinage of Hispania Citerior.* New York 1932.

G. F. Hill: *On the coins of the Narbonensis with Iberian inscriptions.* New York 1930.

J. Millas and F. Mateu: Sobre las inscripciones monetarias punico-hispanas. *Sefarad.* IX (1949) pp. 432–441.

CHAPTER VII *Religion and Ritual*

A. Balil: Representaciones de cabezas-cortadas y cabezas-trofeo en el Levante español. *C.C.P.P.* pp. 871–888.

J. M. Blazquez: Dioses y caballos en el mundo ibérico. *Zephyrus.* V (1954) pp. 193–212.

J. M. Blazquez: Las diosas sagradas de Elche (Alicante). *C.C.P.P.* pp. 747–753.

J. M. Blazquez: La interpretación de la pátera de Tivissa. *Ampurias* XVII–XVIII (1955–1956) pp. 111–140.

J. M. Blazquez: *Religiones primitivas de España. 1. Fuentes literarias y epigraficas.* Madrid 1962.

E. Cuadrado: La diosa ibérica de los caballos. *C.C.P.P.* pp. 797–811.

J. M. de NAVASCUES: El mapa de los hallazgos de epigrafes romanos con nombres de divinidades indigenas en la Peninsula Iberica. *C.N.A.* II (1951) pp. 327–336.

A. FERNANDEZ de AVILES: Relieves hispano-romanos con representaciones ecuestres. *A.E.Arq.* XV (1942) pp. 199–215.

The Sanctuaries:

I. CALVO and J. CABRE: Excavaciones en la cueva y Collado de los Jardines (Santa Elena, Jaén) *J.S.E.A.* (1918 and 1919).

E. CUADRADO: Excavaciones en el santuario ibérico del Cigarralejo (Mula, Murcia). *C.G.E.A.* 21. (1950).

R. LANTIER and J. CABRE: El santuari ibérico del Castellar de Santisteban. *Com. Inv. Pal. y Preh.* Madrid 1917.

C. VISEDO: Excavaciones en La Serreta de Alcoy. *J.S.E.A.* no. 41 1921–1922.

The Cemeteries:

M. ALMAGRO: *Las necropolis de Ampurias.* 11. Barcelona 1955.

G. BONSOR: Les colonies agricoles préromaines de la vallée du Betis. *Rev. Arch.* XXXV, 1899.

J. CABRE and F. MOTOS: La necrópolis ibérica de Tútugi (Galera, prov. de Granada). *J.S.E.A.* no. 25. 1920.

J. CABRE: Arquitectura hispánica: el sepulcro de Toya. *A.E.A.Arq.* I (1925) pp. 73–101.

CERRALBO, MARQUÉS DE: *Las necrópolis ibéricas.* Madrid 1916.

M. LOUIS and O. J. TAFFANEL: *Le premier Age du fer Languedocien.* II. *Les necropoles à incinération.* Bordighera-Montpellier 1958.

G. NIETO: Noticia de las excavaciones realizadas en la necrópolis hispánica del Cabecico del Tesoro de Verdolay, Murcia. *B.S.E.* VI (1939–1940) pp. 137–160; IX (1942–1943) pp. 191–196; X (1943–1944) pp. 165–175.

J. SANCHEZ JIMENEZ: Excavaciones y trabajos arqueológicos en la provincia de Albacete de 1942 a 1946. *C.G.E.A.* 15 (1947).

CHAPTER VIII *Iberian Art*

F. ALVAREZ OSSORIO: *Catálogo de los exvotos de bronce ibéricos del Museo Arqueológico Nacional.* Madrid 1941.

P. BOSCH GIMPERA: Relaciones entre el arte ibérico y el griego. *A.P.L.* I (1928) pp. 163–177.

A. GARCIA BELLIDO: Las relaciones entre el arte etrusco y el ibero. *A.E.A.Arq.* VII (1931) pp. 119–149.

A. GARCIA BELLIDO: Una cabeza ibérica del estilo de las korai aticas. *A.E.A.Arq.* XI (1935) pp. 165–178.

A. GARCIA BELLIDO: Algunos problemas de arte y cronología ibéricos. *A.E.Arq.* (1943) pp. 78–108; pp. 272–299.

A. GARCIA BELLIDO: *Ars Hispaniae.* 1, 2. Madrid 1946.

A. FERNANDEZ DE AVILES: Esculturas del Cerro de los Santos. La Coleción Velasco (Museo Antropológico) en el Museo Arqueologico Nacional. *A.E.Arq.* XVI (1943) pp. 361–387.

R. LANTIER: *Bronzes votifs ibériques.* Paris 1935.

CHAPTER IX *Pottery*

M. ALMAGRO: El estado actual de la clasificación de la cerámica ibérica. *C.A.S.E.* Alcoy (1950) pp. 128–144.

I. BALLESTER and others: *Cerámica del Cerro de San Miguel de Liria.* *C.V.H.* Madrid 1954.

J. CABRE: *Cerámica de Azaila. C.V.H.* Madrid 1944.

E. CUADRADO: Materiales ibéricos: cerámica roja de procedencia incierta. *Zephyrus.* IV (1953) pp. 265–309.

E. CUADRADO: Las primeras aportaciones del Cigarralejo al problema de la cronología ibérica. *C.A.S.E.* Alcoy (1950) pp. 159–172.

A. DEL CASTILLO: La cerámica ibérica de Ampurias. Cerámica del Sudeste. *A.E.Arq.* XVI (1943) pp. 1–48.

D. FLETCHER: Sobre la cronología de la cerámica ibérica. *A.E.Arq.* XVI (1943) pp. 109–115.

A. GARCIA BELLIDO: Problemas de la cronología ibérica. *Saitabi.* II (1944) pp. 109–119.

A. GARCIA BELLIDO: La pintura mayor entre los iberos. *A.E.Arq.* XVIII (1945) pp. 250–257.

A. Garcia Bellido: Nuevos datos sobre la cronología final de la cerámica ibérica y sobre su expansión extrapeninsular. *A.E.Arq.* XXV (1952) pp. 39–45.

A. Garcia Bellido: Estado actual del problema referente a la expansion de la cerámica ibérica por la cuenca occidental del Mediterráneo. *A.E.Arq.* XXX (1957) pp. 90–106.

CHAPTER X *Tartessian-Iberian Jewellery*

A. Blanco: Orientalia. Estudio de objetos fenicios y orientalizantes en la peninsula. *A.E.Arq.* XXIX (1956) pp. 3–51.

J. de M. Carriazo: Gold of Tarshish? *I.L.N.* 31. 1. 1959. No. 6243.

E. Cuadrado: La fíbula hispánica y sus problemas. *Zephyrus.* VIII (1957) pp. 5–76.

W. L. Hildburgh: A find of ibero-roman silver at Cordova (tesoro de Marrubial). *Archaeologia.* LXXII (1921–1922) pp. 161–184.

J. Maluquer: Un interesante lote de bronces, hallados en el castro de Sanchorreja (Avila). *Zephyrus.* VII (1957) pp. 241–256.

J. Maluquer: Nuevos hallazgos en el area tartésica. *Zephyrus.* IX (1958) pp. 201–219.

References to many of the Spanish treasures not listed individually in the bibliography will be found in *A.E.Arq.,* notably in the volumes for the years 1936, 1937, 1943, 1953, 1956, 1957, and 1959.

Sources of Illustrations

It is my pleasant duty to thank the following official bodies and private individuals who have allowed me to use their negatives or lent me prints for the plates in this book:

National Archaeological Museum of Madrid: 1, 2, 3, 5, 10, 17, 18, 21, 22, 23, 24, 25, 28, 39, 41, 44, 45, 46, 47, 51, 54, 56, 57, 61, 79; Barcelona, Archaeological Museum: 14, 15, 16, 19, 20, 26, 40, 42, 53, 59, 60, 65, 66, 67, 68, 69, 71, 72, 73, 74, 80, 81; Arxiu Mas, Barcelona: 4, 55, 75, 76, 77; Sr Emeterio Cuadrado, Madrid: 34, 35, 36, 37, 38; Albacete Archaeological Museum (Sr J. Jiménez Sánchez): 8, 9, 50, 58;

Murcia Archaeological Museum (Sr M. Jorge Aragoneses): 11, 62. Deutsches Archaologisches Institut, Madrid: 12, 13; Prof. J. de Mata Carriazo, Seville: 6, 7; Seville Archaeological Museum (Miss C. Fernández Chicarro): 48, 52; Elche Museum (Sr Ramos Folqués): 63, 64; Prof. J. Maluquer de Motes, Barcelona: 27; Alicante Archaeological Museum (Sr J. Lafuente): 43; Junta de Museos Municipales, Barcelona: 78; Centro Excursionista de Santa Coloma de Gramanet (Sr de la Vega): 90; Sr Xavier Calicó, Barcelona: 82a; Sr Leandro Villaronga, Barcelona: 82b–89; Photographs numbers 29, 30, 31, 32, 33, 49 were taken by the author.

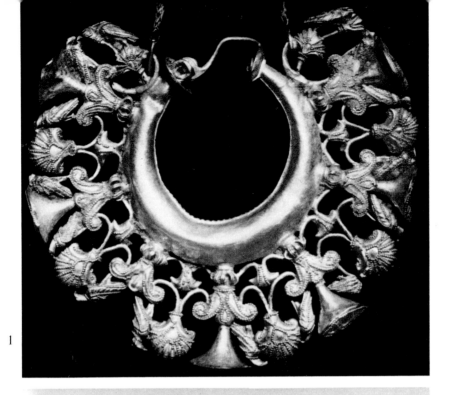

1

2

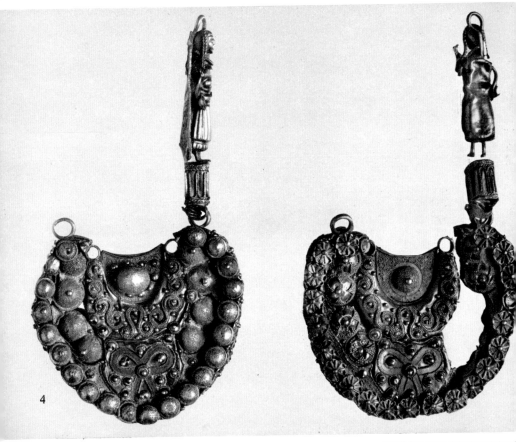

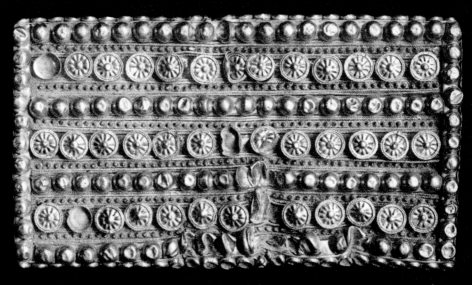

8 9

10

11

12

13

14

15   16

17

18

19

20

21

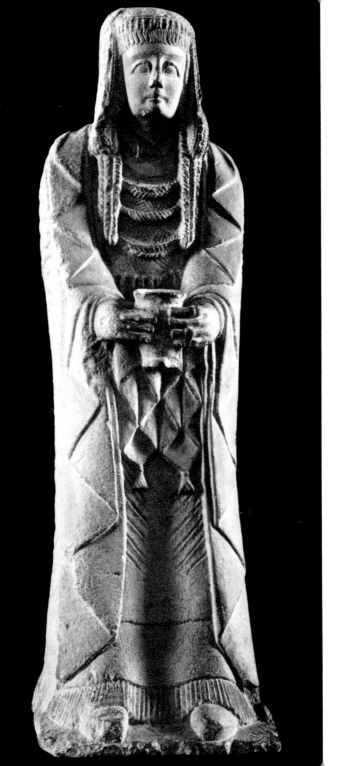

23

24

25

26

27

28

29

30

31

32

35

36

37

39   40

1

42

43

44

45

46

47

48

49

51

3

54

55

56

58

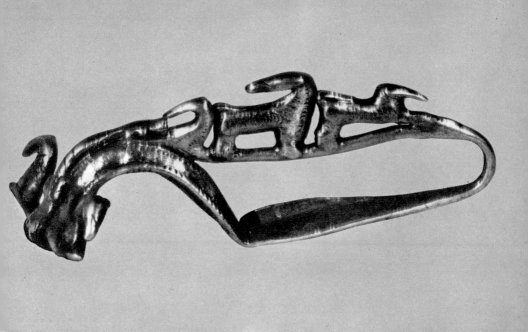

59

60

61

62

63

64

65

70

71

73

74

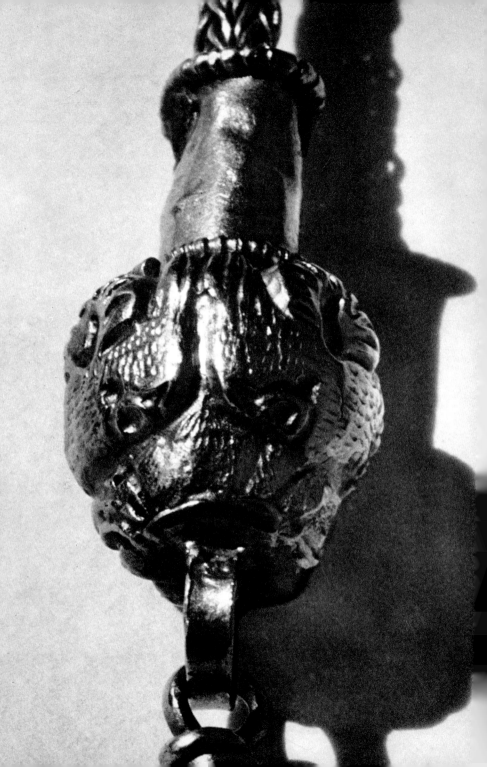

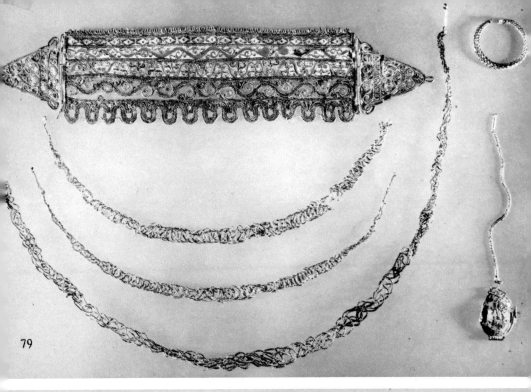

79

80

81

82

a   *b*

83

a   *b*

84

a   *b*

85

a   *b*

86 *a*

b

87

88 *a*

b

89 *a*

b

Notes on the Plates

1 Gold ear-ring, ornamented with alternating lotus flowers and palmettes flanked by inward-facing representations of the sacred vulture. Diam. 7 cm., weight 36·30 gr. (its twin weighs 27·50 gr.). It forms part of the famous treasure of La Aliseda (30 km. from Caceres) discovered in 1920. National Archaeological Museum, Madrid.

2 Clasp and portion of belt from La Aliseda. Gold. Total length 63 cm. The two outer strips of the two rectangular plaques of the clasp are decorated with a motif of a man fighting a lion, the centre strip with opposed palmettes, repoussé with a granulated background. The rest of the belt comprises 35 square plaques (2 × 1 cm.) depicting the same man-and-lion motif and 21 plaques (and three fragments) bearing a sphinx and three lotus flowers. The plaques have a slender chain as border.

3 Detail of one of two gold bracelets from La Aliseda, 6 cm. in diameter and weighing 56·30 and 56·25 gr. respectively. A double row of continuous spirals in openwork constitutes the main decoration. The ends have palmettes on a granulated background.

4 Gold ear-rings from Santiago de la Espada. Length 12 cm., max. diam. 7 cm. The closest parallels are provided by the winged Damas of Elche, but the metalwork is typically Tartessian. Instituto Valencia de Don Juan, Madrid.

5 Gold diadem from La Aliseda. Length 20 cm., weight 60 gr. It consists of numerous articulated pieces in filigree-work forming a band of rosettes and garlands, with a fringe of spherules on short chains. The fasteners are triangular in shape. In the hollows of the rosettes traces of paste are still visible, while a turquoise still occupies one of them. National Archaeological Museum, Madrid.

6　Pieces of jewellery from the gold treasure found at El Carambolo, near Seville, in 1959. All told, the treasure comprises 21 items of 24 carat gold weighing 2,950 gr. (94·843 oz. Troy). Archaeological Museum, Seville.

7　One of four large 24-carat gold plaques, having a regular pattern of semi-spheres, rosettes and fillets. 11 × 6 cm. From El Carambolo. Archaeological Museum, Seville.

8, 9　The Sphinx of Haches (Bogarra, Albacete). Casual find in 1946. Soft whitish sandstone. The winged sphinx on a smooth plinth forming an integral part of it has its head turned towards the right. Total height 70 cm. Archaeological Museum, Albacete.

10　The Beast of Balazote (prov. of Albacete), found at the end of last century. The head was made, and found, as a separate piece. Total height 73 cm., length of base 92 cm., width at base 37 cm. National Archaeological Museum, Madrid.

11　Limestone head from the cemetery of Cabecico de Verdolay (prov. of Murcia). It was found close to the torso with which it has been coupled to form the 'Seated Lady of Verdolay' (see fig. 46), but the two parts may not have belonged to the same figure. The massive head has the hair arranged very symmetrically. Height 18 cm. Archaeological Museum, Murcia.

12, 13　Head of a *kore* from a site in the Southeast or East of the Peninsula (?Alicante). Soft white limestone. Height 24 cm. The head-dress is similar to that worn by the Sphinx of Agost. Archaeological Museum, Barcelona.

14　Body and wing of sphinx from Villaricos. The head and lower extremities are missing. Length 87 cm., height 36 cm. National Archaeological Museum, Madrid.

15　Damaged cist of polychrome limestone. From Tomb 76 of the cemetery of Tutugi (Galera, prov. of Granada). The plate shows the right-hand side decorated with a black griffin on a red background and accessory geometric patterns. The front of this cist is shown in fig. 39. Length 41 cm., width 32 cm., height 28 cm. National Archaeological Museum, Madrid.

16 Pyxis decorated with two friezes of concentric circles separated by a band of excised lozenges. The handle of the lid is in the form of a dove. From Peal de Becerro (prov. of Jaén). Height 10 cm., total length (with lid) 16 cm. National Archaeological Museum, Madrid.

17 Attic krater found in Tomb 83 of cemetery at Tutugi (Galera, prov. of Granada). Painted by the Black Thyrsos painter (375–350 B.C.). Height 32 cm., diam. at lip 32 cm. From the Motos Collection, National Archaeological Museum, Madrid.

18 Native krater used as a cinerary urn. Local imitation of the Attic column kraters. Found in the cemetery of Almedinilla (prov. of Córdoba). Height 31 cm., diam. at lip 17 cm. National Archaeological Museum, Madrid.

19 Red-varnished pot with decoration of bands and a frieze of impressed rosettes. From the cemetery of Almedinilla. Height 19 cm., diam. at lip 18 cm. National Archaeological Museum, Madrid.

20 Globular vase with high conical neck and handles, decorated with painted bands. From the cemetery of Peal de Becerro (prov. of Jaén). Height 28 cm., diam. at lip 13 cm. National Archaeological Museum, Madrid.

21 Alabaster statuette of the Goddess of Fertility. She is seated on a backless chair and flanked by two sphinxes. From her perforated breasts liquid could be made to flow into the bowl she holds. From Tomb 20 of the cemetery of Tutugi (Galera, prov. of Granada). Height 17·8 cm., width 10·6 cm., depth 12·7 cm. National Archaeological Museum, Madrid.

22 The magnificent Dama of El Cerro de los Santos (prov. of Albacete). Porous limestone with burnt yellow patina. Traces of polychrome painting (red on lips, mantilla and cloak). Height 1·35 m. National Archaeological Museum, Madrid.

23 The Dama de Elche. This masterpiece of Iberian sculpture was found in August 1897 in La Alcudia de Elche and was bought for 4,000 francs by P. Paris for the Louvre where it was placed on exhibition in December of that year. During the German occupation of France it was kept in the castle of Montauban. In February 1941 it was returned to Spain together with the greater portion of the Osuna sculptures by the Petain Government. Height 56 cm., width across face between inner edges of the 'wheel' head-dress 19 cm., actual diam. of 'wheels' 19·5 cm. Prado Museum, Madrid.

24 Architectural fragment (? column capital) from Elche. Found in 1899 near the place where the Dama de Elche was discovered. Total height 49 cm. National Archaeological Museum, Madrid.

25 Capital from the Cortijo del Ahorcado, Baeza (prov. of Jaén). Found on a limestone shaft. Length 60 cm., height 40 cm. National Archaeological Museum, Madrid.

26 Iron bit. The interlinked central bar was held in place in the horse's mouth by crescent-shaped side-pieces. From Almedinilla (prov. of Córdoba). Total length 33 cm. National Archaeological Museum, Madrid.

27 The 'Carriazo Bronze', thought to be the cheek-piece of a bit. Bought in the antique market, it almost certainly derives from the province of Seville. Height 9·5 cm., original width 16·20 cm. (now 15·30 cm.). Arch. Mus. Seville, formerly Carriazo Collection, Seville.

28 Silver damascened hilt of a falchion. From Almedinilla (prov. of Córdoba). Length of blade 52 cm. Length of hilt 11·5 cm. National Archaeological Museum, Madrid.

29 The 'Cazurro Vase', one of the most curious examples of Iberian pottery painting. Found in one of the cemeteries of Ampurias (prov. of Gerona). Much restored. Height 26 cm., diam. at lip 15 cm., max. diam. 30 cm. Archaeological Museum, Barcelona.

30–33 The walled enclosure of the habitation site of Ullastret (prov. of Gerona).
30. Entrance gateway, taken from inside. 31. A length of wall and one
of the circular towers. 32. Group of buildings immediately inside the
wall. 33. Partial view of a group of buildings in the sector near the
entrance gateway.

34 Air view of the Sanctuary of El Cigarralejo in the *vega* of the River Mula
(prov. of Murcia).

35 One of the most delicately wrought votive offerings from the Sanctuary
of El Cigarralejo (Mula, prov. of Murcia). Small sandstone horse, its
curved neck and short head giving an effect of harmony. The bridle and
trappings are indicated. The great number of horses found in this sanctuary constitutes one of the most sensational discoveries made since 1945.
All the figurines are small, between 10–15 cm. long. This particular
specimen measures 19 × 11·5 × 4·5 cm. Sr E. Cuadrado Collection,
Madrid.

36 Bifacial sandstone relief from El Cigarralejo depicting a horse with
thick body, short concave back and broad convex rump. A similar
horse appears on the reverse. 11 × 8 × 4 cm. Sr E. Cuadrado collection, Madrid.

37 Sandstone relief of a she-ass and foal from El Cigarralejo. Note that the
contours of the relief are bevelled. 15·2 × 8 × 3 cm. Sr E. Cuadrado
Collection, Madrid.

38 Detail of sandstone horse's head with trappings and bridle. This is
generally acknowledged to be the finest head in Iberian art by 'The
Master of El Cigarralejo'. From El Cigarralejo. Sr E. Cuadrado Collection, Madrid.

39 Dama offering a dove. Bronze votive-offering in the finest style of the
sanctuary of Despeñaperros (prov. of Jaén). Height 13·5 cm. National
Archaeological Museum, Madrid.

R*

40 Well-made small bronze horse showing saddle and harness from the sanctuary of El Palmar (Murcia). Height 7·8 cm. Archaeological Museum, Barcelona.

41 Three bronze votive offerings from the sanctuary of Despeñaperros. The left-hand man wears a short tunic and carries a fruit in his right hand and an unidentified object in his left. Height 10 cm. National Archaeological Museum, Madrid, inventory no. 28948. The centre figure stands in the attitude of prayer, no. 28926. The right-hand figure is a naked man wearing only a belt and with open hands. Height 10·8 cm., no. 29001.

42 Relief of 'The Tamer'. The central figure is that of a two-faced male figure seated between two rearing horses. From Villaricos. Height 30 cm., width 38 cm., maximum thickness 17 cm. Archaeological Museum, Barcelona.

43 Limestone relief from a woman's tomb in the cemetery of La Albufereta (prov. of Alicante). A woman is depicted standing spinning opposite a warrior who leans on his lance. Height 17 cm. Archaeological Museum, Alicante.

44 Male and female *consort* offerers jointly holding a large vase of gifts before them. From El Cerro de los Santos (prov. of Albacete). Height 64 cm. National Archaeological Museum, Madrid, no. 3508.

45 Female head with mitre head-dress from El Cerro de los Santos. A masterpiece of native workmanship. Height 41·5 cm. National Archaeological Museum, Madrid, no. 7510. (Cast of original in Perelada.)

46 Sculpture of an offering Dama of unequal proportions. The square head crushes the too-narrow shoulders and the fingers are mis-shapen. From El Cerro de los Santos. Height 59 cm. National Archaeological Museum, Madrid, no. 7624.

47 Dama of massive aspect seated on a backless throne. The hairstyle of zigzags and a narrow band shows beneath the huge turban-like mitre.

From El Cerro de los Santos. Height 70 cm. National Archaeological Museum, Madrid, no. 7627.

48 Headless seated male and female figures from Cortijo de Tixe (Torre de los Herberos, Dos Hermanas, prov. of Seville). The man wears the Iberian *sagum* although the garments and footwear are of the Roman period. Height 1·60 m. Archaeological Museum, Seville.

49 Male head in soft white limestone, from El Cerro de los Santos. Height 25 cm. Archaeological Museum, Barcelona.

50 Limestone male head, the left side very much destroyed, from El Tolmo de Minateda (prov. of Albacete). Chance find 1929. Height 26 cm. Archaeological Museum, Albacete.

51 Male head from El Cerro de los Santos (prov. of Albacete). The schematized treatment of the hair provides a startling contrast with the freedom of execution of the features. Height 22 cm. National Archaeological Museum, Madrid, no. 7513.

52 Stone relief from Osuna showing a hind and her fawn with a palm tree behind. 1903 excavations. Height 60 cm., width 47 cm., thickness 10 cm. Municipal Collection of Archaeological Museum, Seville.

53 The 'Lioness' (bull) of Sagunto (prov. of Valencia). Height 80 cm. Sagunto Museum.

54 Limestone bull from Osuna at one time embedded in a wall. Length 1·10 m., height 65 cm. National Archaeological Museum, Madrid.

55 The Osuna flute player. A limestone corner-stone from Osuna depicting a flute player (*auletris*) on one side and a man wearing a cape upon the other. 59 × 45 cm. National Archaeological Museum, Madrid.

56 Limestone corner-stone from Osuna, in two fragments, showing a boy rider on a horse. Dimensions 74 × 74 cm. National Archaeological Museum, Madrid.

57 The horn player of Osuna. Carved on two separate blocks of limestone. Height 110 cm. × 57 cm. National Archaeological Museum, Madrid.

58 'Vase of the Dragons' from tomb 52, cemetery of Hoya de Santa Ana (prov. of Albacete). Made of black burnished clay and used as a funerary urn, found with the bones in it. Height 16·5 cm. Archaeological Museum, Albacete.

59 Silver fibula from the treasure of Los Almadenes de Pozoblanco (prov. of Córdoba). Length 10 cm. Archaeological Museum, Córdoba.

60 Damascened belt clasp with stylized vegetable and meander patterns. From Peal de Becerro (Tugia). Height 11 cm., minimum width 11 cm. National Archaeological Museum, Madrid.

61 'Vase of the Warriors' from cemetery of Archena (prov. of Murcia). When found it contained cremated remains. Height 40 cm. Maximum diameter 35·6 cm., width of opening 31·2 cm. National Archaeological Museum, Madrid.

62 'Vase of the Goats', one of the most realistic products of Iberian painting. From the cemetery of El Cabecico del Tesoro de Verdolay (prov. of Murcia). Height 20 cm., diameter of lip 11 cm. Archaeological Museum, Murcia.

63 Lid of the urn, shown in Plate 64, decorated with stylized floral patterns. From the cemetery of Oliva (prov. of Valencia). Height 20 cm., maximum diameter 40 cm. Archaeological Museum, Barcelona.

64 Urn of red clay decorated with stylized floral patterns which contained two bronze armlets, two circular plaques, a belt buckle, a fibula, and fragments of an 'Hellenistic' cup. From the cemetery of Oliva (prov. of Valencia). Height 55 cm. Archaeological Museum, Barcelona.

65 Detail of decoration of an urn from the cemetery of Oliva (Valencia)

with warriors. It contained cremated remains. Archaeological Museum, Barcelona.

66 Detail from the same urn, perhaps depicting the scaling of a city's walls.

67 'Vase of the Winged Goddess' from Elche, decorated with stylized floral patterns. Height 52 cm. Municipal Museum, Elche.

68 'La Pepona de Elche'. A rare specimen of Iberian frontal art in vase painting. Height 48 cm. Municipal Museum, Elche.

69 *Kalathos* (or top-hat) shaped vase, decorated with two friezes of intersecting concentric semicircles. From the habitation site of Sidamunt (prov. of Lérida). Height 24 cm. Archaeological Museum, Barcelona.

70 Entrance gateway with flanking towers of the habitation site of El Castellet de Banyoles de Tivissa (prov. of Tarragona).

71 Two silver vases (6·3 cm. and 6·8 cm. high) shaped like that carried by the offerers from El Cerro de los Santos (Plate 44). The right-hand one has an inscription in Iberian. From Tivissa (prov. of Tarragona). Archaeological Museum, Barcelona.

72 Silver vase with repoussé patterns of meanders, rope-twists, leaves and fruit. From Tivissa (prov. of Tarragona). Height 9 cm. Barcelona Archaeological Museum.

73 Silver patera (dish) with a wolf's head in high relief on the boss. From Tivissa. Diameter 15·6 cm. Archaeological Museum, Barcelona.

74 Silver patera with appliqué gold leaf, chiselled and depicting votive and funerary scenes. The lion's head on the boss is separately soldered on. There is a circular Iberian inscription on the reverse. From Tivissa. Diameter 17 cm. Archaeological Museum, Barcelona.

75 Silver-gilt diadem (or belt ornament) with repoussé patterns of flowers, rosettes, palmettes and a border of running spirals. From the 1917 Mogón

hoard (prov. of Jaén), which was contained in a pot covered with a cake of melted-down silver. With it were armlets, bracelets, a plaque from a dagger sheath, a clasp, a gorgon-head medallion and 1,258 coins of 89 B.C. National Archaeological Museum, Madrid.

76 Silver repoussé work plaque used as a casing for a dagger sheath. The square panel shows a horse and the triangular panel a deer, a fish and a bird. From the Mogón hoard. Length 19 cm. National Archaeological Museum, Madrid.

77 Silver belt clasp depicting a bird with outstretched wings. From the Mogón hoard. Diameter 8 cm. National Archaeological Museum, Madrid.

78 Lion's head on the gold necklace from Valleta del Valeroso (Soses, Serós, prov. of Lérida). The necklace consisted of a chain of plaited gold threads 32·5 cm. long, ending in this head and a clasp hook. Archaeological Museum, Lérida.

79 The treasure of Jávea (Alicante), consisting of a filigree diadem with repoussé and plaited decorations forming Hellenistic style spirals, two slender chains which hung from the diadem (one with a small end gem), a silver armlet and fragments of others. National Archaeological Museum, Madrid.

80 Limestone block with a long Iberian inscription. From Santa Perpetua de la Moguda (prov. of Barcelona). Height 102 cm., width 50 cm., thickness 29 cm. Archaeological Museum, Barcelona.

81 Sandstone stela of a rider with a shield and a frieze of lances. From Palermo (Caspe, prov. of Saragossa). Height 128 cm., width 69 cm., thickness 22 cm. Archaeological Museum, Barcelona.

82 Iberian silver coins from Catalonia: a. Ildirda-Salirban, b. Ausescen.

83 Silver drachmas of a. Emporion, b. Arse.

84–86 Silver denarii from Catalonia, the Ebro Valley and Andalusia. 84a. Cese, b. Ildirda; 85a. Icaloscen, b. Bolscan; 86a. Arecorada, b. Turiasu.

87–89 Bronze asses. 87. Emporion (Undicescen); 88a. Lauro, b. Ildirda; 89a. Cese, b. Saldiue.

90 Iron firedog of La Tène style with bull's-head ends. From the dwelling site of Puig Castellar (Santa Coloma de Gramanet, prov. of Barcelona). Length 1·25 m., height 38·7 cm. Santa Coloma de Gramanet Museum.

Index

Abdera, 52
Abella, 43
Abengibre treasure, 187
Acebuchal, 46
  tumuli, 151
Agde, 21
agriculture, 30–31, 119–124
Agrippa, 192
Agullana, cemetery, 41, 43, 46
Akra Leuke, 53, 54, 58, 99, 110
Alalia, Battle of, 17, 51, 53
Albacete, 58
  cemetery, 142
Albaida, 99
Albuferata,
  inscriptions, 91
  sculpture, 158, 162
Albuñol, 67
Alcacer do Sol, 181
Alcantarilla, 46
  graves, 151
Aliseda belt, 133, 179–180
Alloza, vases, 77, 79, 174–177
Almagro, Martin, 27
Almedinalla, 126
  cemetery, 23, 81, 144
  falchion from, 125
Alonai, 53
Alparatus, 45
alphabets, 87–96, 131
Amarejo, 111
amphorae, 144
Ampurdan, 100

Ampurias, 28, 100
  pottery, 169, 174–175
Amusicus, 118
Andalusia, 34, 38, 45–47, 50, 126
  Lower, 15
  Southeast, 15, 38
  Upper, 15, 35
Andosini, 31, 100
Anseresa, 109
Antequera, 35
Antiochus of Syracuse, 191
Appian, 38
d'Arbois de Jubainville, 23
Archena, 26, 59, 75
  figurine, 82
  pottery, 169
architectural sculpture, 155–156
architecture, 97–115, 149
Arcobriga cemetery, 81
Arenosi, 31, 100
Arganthonios, King, 49, 52
Aristophanes, 191
arrowheads, 43
art, 41, 151–164
Artemidorus, 192
Asclepiades, 192
Ascoli Bronze, 62, 96
astral cults, 131
Atlantic Bronze Age, 49
Attenes, *regulus turdetanorum*, 116
Aulus Gelius, 36
Ausa, 97
Ausescen, 128

Ausetani, 31, 75, 100, 118
Avienus, 22, 26, 46, 131, 190–191
axe moulds, 43
axes, Bronze Age, 43, 50, 63
Azaila, painted vases, 172–174

Baebelo, mine shaft, 122
Baena, cemetery, 144
Baetica, 34, 38
Balazote, 58
Balones, stone beast, 158
Bargusi, 100
Barquidae, 129
Barranco Hondo, 45
Basques, 22
Bastetani, 34, 39, 142
'Bastetanian Dance' vase, 171
Basti, cemetery, 45, 144
Bastida de les Alcuses, chain from, 188
Baza, 59
beakers, 42
Beast of Balozote, 156
belt, Aliseda, 133, 180
   from Sanchorreja, 186
Beltram, P. and A., 28
Belli, 34
Bencarron, 46
Besadin, 117
Blazquez, J. M., 28
Blockstil, 158
Bonsor, G., 23, 151
Bosch Gimpera, P., 24–26
breastplate, from Carambolo treasure, 102–103
brewing, 124
Bronze Age, 43, 44

bronze,
   Ascoli, 62
   braserillos, 181
   brooches, 72
   hoards, 43
   oenochoai, 51, 181
   sculptures, 163–164
   weapons, 50
brooches, 72–73
Brythons, 27
Budar, 117
bull-cult, 131
burial customs, 40, 44, 137–151
Burriach, 97, 104

Cabezo de Alcalá de Azaila, 109
Cabezo de Monleón de Caspe, 28, 43, 44, 105
   grave, 141
Cabrera de Mataró, 126
   cemetery, 140
   cups from, 178
Caesar, 119
caetratus, 73
Caldero de Qurenima, 45
Caldetas, 104
Camallera, swords from, 83
Can Montmany de Palleja, 43
Cañada de Ruiz Sanchez, 46
Cánovas Head, 160
Cantabri, 62
Cape Artemision, 52
Capo Soprano de Gela, 104
Capsian, 25
Carambolo treasures, 47, 50
Caravaca, 59
Carmona, 23, 47, 50, 114

ivories, 189
   pottery, 168
Carpentania, 120
Carriazo bronze, 133
Cartagena, 58, 122
Carthage, 47, 53–54, 57
Carthago Nova, 99
carts, 63, 84
Cassiterides, 53
Castell de la Fosca, 101, 102
Castellvell, 109
Castillar de Santisban, 136
Castulo, 155
Catalonia, 15, 16, 25, 31, 38, 42, 56–58,
   99–105, 119
Cato, 110, 119, 123
cattle-breeders, 118
Caudete, stone stags from, 157, 158
Cayla de Mailhac, 28
   cemetery, 139
Cazurro vase, 67, 176–177
Ceal,
   cemetery, 149
   pottery, 168
Celtes, 191
Celtiberians, 36, 75
Celtic influence, 46
   on jewellery, 186
Cerralbo, Marquis de, 23
Cerratani, 31, 100
Cerro de los Santos, 23, 68, 136
   sculptures from, 158–160
Cerro del Trigo, 114
Cese, 128
Chalcidia, 51
chariots, 84
Charpolar, 110

Cheste, hoard, 54
Chorographia, 192
Cilbiceni, 21
cinnibar mining, 122
city-state system, 118
climate, 36
clothing, 63, 66–68
Cogotas, 46
coins, 57, 78, 80, 94, 127–130, 187
Colaius of Samos, 17, 49, 51, 52, 191
Coll del Moro, grave, 140
Contestani, 34, 62, 110, 142
copper mines, 50
Corribilio, *nobilis rex de Licabrum,* 116
Cortes, 105
Cortes de Navarra, 28, 41
Cortijo del Ahorcado, 155
Cossetani, 31, 100
Costitx, stone bulls, 158
Cova d'Or, 44
Covalta, 26, 99
crafts and craftsmen, 124–126
cremation, 41, 61, 138, 142
Cruz del Negro, tumuli, 151
Cueva de la Sarsa, 44
Culchas, *regulus,* 116, 117
Cypsela, 53, 54, 103

daggers,
   antenna, 83
   double globular, 83
Dama de Elche, 23, 26, 68, 71, 160, 184
dancing, 64–65
Deitani, 34, 142
Demeter, statue, 131
Despeñaperros, 78
devotio, 119

diadem from Aliseda, 180–181
  from Jávea, 188
Diodorus, 78, 124, 191
Dionysus, 73
dove-worship, 132

Ebro valley, 15, 16, 25, 31–34, 37, 43–44,
  58–60, 105–110, 118–119
Ebussus, 129
Edeca, 118
Edecon, 118
Edetani, 34, 118, 142
El Acebuchal, 50
El Argar period, 40, 44
El Boverot urnfield, 142
El Cabeccio del Tesoro de Verdolay, 26
  cemetery, 142, 143
  seated stone figures, 158
El Cabezo del Tio Pio de Archena, 111
El Carambolo, 114
  pottery, 168
  treasure, 182–185
El Cigarralejo, 26, 28, 133, 137, 142, 155
  pottery, 165
  reliefs, 84, 85, 91, 162
El Collado de los Jardines, 24, 112, 136
El Llano de la Consolación, 24, 136
  cemetery, 142
  sculptures from, 158
El Molar, cemetery, 142
El Tomlo de Minateda, sculpture, 160
Elbysinians, 191
Elche, 58, 133, 155
  Dama de, 23, 26, 68, 71, 72, 160, 184
  pottery, 132, 134, 169
Els Castellans, 105, 109
Els Espleters, 142

Emporion, 52, 53, 56–58, 97, 99, 100,
  124, 127, 128, 140, 191
Ensérune, 28, 97
  cemetery, 139
  graffiti, 94–96
Ephorus, 22, 51, 67, 191
Eratosthenes, 47, 192
Erythia island, 190
Escodines Altes, 108
Escodines, Baixes, 108
esparto production, 124
Ethiopians, 191
Etmanei, 21
Etnologia de la Península Ibérica, 25
Etruscans, 53
Evora treasure, 184–186

falarica, 80, 81
falcate, 82
falchions, 81, 82–83, 125, 143
falx, 83
fibulae, 50
fishing, 64, 121–122
flax, 124
flora, *see* vegetation
flute, 64
forum, 111
fruit growing, 120–121

Gades, 47, 52, 99, 116, 129, 131
Galba, 62
Galera, 59
  grave, 145, 147, 148
Galicia, 49
Garcia Bellido, A., 26, 29, 152
Gargoris, King, 49
Gela, 51

geology, 30
Gerunda, 97
Geryon, King, 48, 190
Gimeno, J., 28
gladius hispaniensis, 82
Goidels, 27
gold,
    jewellery, 182–186
    mines, 123
    smiths, 127
Gomez Moreno, Prof. M., 25, 90–92
graffiti, 94–96, 176
grain, 119–120
Gran Dama del Cerro, 70, 71, 160
Granada, 35
Greeks, 49–51
Guadalquivir valley, 34, 35, 37, 38, 45,
    111–115, 120
Guadina river, 50
Guadix, 35, 59
Gymnetes, 21

Hallstatt cultures, 40–41, 42, 44, 46, 105,
    109, 139
Hamilcar, 54
Hannibal, 17, 54, 57, 62, 65, 75, 80, 111,
    117, 119, 122
Hanno, 191
Hasdrubal, 117
Hathor, 133
head-dresses, 69
Hecateus, 21, 22
Hellanicus of Lesbos, 191
helmet, 78
    Corinthian, 52
Hemeroskopeion, 17, 52, 58, 99, 110
    destruction, 54

Heracleia, 52
Heracles, 49
Heraclids, 47
Herodorus of Heraklea, 191
Herodotus, 53, 191
Hesiod, 190
Hesperides, 190
Himera, 17
    battle, 73
Himilcon, 191
horse-burials, 141
horse-goddess, 84
horses and horsemanship, 84–87, 121
houses, 63, 97–115
Huelva estuary dredging, 50
    hoard, 50, 52
Hugelgräberkultur, 141
Humboldt, Alexander von, 22
hunting, 64
Hyères Islands, 51
Hyops, 53

Ibiza, 17, 52
Ileates, 21
Ilergetes, 17, 34, 74, 100, 118
Ilipa, silver mines, 122
Illyrians, 27
incineration, 16
Indibil, 62, 75
Indica, 97, 99
Indicetes, 31, 97, 100
inscriptions, 88, 91, 139, 172
Intitut d'Estudis Catalans, 24
intervallum, 111
ironworking, 41, 123
Isaiah, 49
Isis, 133

ivory,
  combs, 46, 189
  plaques, 46, 189

javelin, 80, 81
jewellery, 69–73, 144, 154, 157, 179–189
Josefina, cave, 42
Juan Abad hoard, 188
Junta Superior de Excavaciones y Anti-
    guedades, 24

Kallipolis, 53
Kamina, inscription, 88
Kelkianians, 191
kilns, 166–167
Kinetes, 191
Kotinai, 122

La Aliseda treasure, 179–181
La Bastida de Mogente, 26, 28, 110–111
  plan, 112–113
La Creuata, 99, 102
La Guardia, graves, 150–151, 156, 157
La Hoya de Santa Ana, 28
  cemetery, 142, 143, 165
La Luz, 24
  figurines, 164
La Pedrera de Balaguer, cemeteries, 28, 43,
    100, 109, 141
La Serreta de Alcoy, 24, 99, 110, 137
  lead inscription, 91, 92
  terracottas, 163
La Viña de Marisparza, cemetery, 142
Lacetani, 100
Laietani, 31, 100
lamps, Punic, 144
lance, 80, 81

Languedoc, 55
latifundia, 35
Le Cayla, 46
lead, 91, 92, 95
Lebedontia, 53
Leite de Vasconcelos, 23
Les Ombries de Calaceite, 105, 109
Ligurians, 22
Linares, 58
Liria, 26, 110–111
  painted inscriptions, 172
  pottery, 170–171
  'Vase of the Warriors', 75–76
  vase painting, 77, 170–172
Livy, 61, 64, 73, 80–81, 82, 97, 100, 123,
    193
Los Almandenes de Pozoblanco hoard,
    187
Los Castellones de Ceal, cemetery, 28, 45,
    144, 149, 168
Los Millares culture, 44
Los Monegros, 31
Lubke, Meyer, 26
lunar cults, 131
Lusitania, 49
Lusitanians, 36, 75, 78–79, 138
Luxinius, 'Lord of Carmona', 116, 117

Maestrazgo, 34
Magna Graecia, 50
Mainake, 17, 52
Mairena, 23
Malaca, 52
Mandonius, 62, 75
Marlés, 100
Marseilles, 51
Martial, 37, 61, 63, 120

Martinez Santa Olalla, 27
Mas de Madalenes de Cretas, 105
Massieni, 21
Massilia, 17, 52, 55
Massiliot coin types, 127
Massiliot Sailing Book, 21, 190
Mastreni, 34, 191
Mateu, F., 28
Meca, 111
megalithic cultures, 40, 42, 45
Mélida, J. R., 23
Melkart, 49
Menendez Pidal, R., 26, 27
mercenaries, Iberians as, 73, 191
Meseta, 17
metalwork, 124–126, 152
Minatada, 99
mining and metallurgy, 40, 117, 122–123
Mogente, 99
Mogón hoard, 54, 187
Molá, 46
Molino de Marrubial hoard, 70, 187
Montgó hoard, 54
Monumenta Linguae Ibericae, 22
Murcia, 58
    cemetery, 142
music, 64

nature worship, 135
naukleroi, 52
Navascues, J. M. de, 28
Naxos, 51
necklace from Carambolo, 183–185
Nobilior, 36
Numancia, 17, 24, 25, 38
    destruction, 192

Oestrymnides, islands, 49
Oliva, cemetery, 142
olive production, 120
oppidum, 97
Orbis Pictus, 192
Oretani, 35
Organyá hoard, 43
Orihuela, 58
Oringis, siege, 83
Orke, 129
ostrich egg shells, painted, 144
Osuna, 23, 114
    sculptures from, 26, 65, 68, 69, 75, 76–77, 79–80, 158, 161–162

Palaiapolis, 53
Pallantia, 38
Parazuelos, 45
Paris, P., 23
Penibaetica, 34, 35
Periplus of Avienus, 22, 26, 49, 52, 190
Perotitos *paterae,* 134
Philistos, 22
Philo, 125
Phoenicians, 17, 47–49
pigs, 121
pike, 81
Pindar, 53, 191
Piuro del Barranc Fondo, 25
pit-burials, 42, 44
Pliny the Elder, 39, 49, 192–193
ploughs, 63
Plutarch, 73, 119
Polybius, 21, 61, 74, 192
Pomponius Mela, 192–193
pomegranates, 120, 121
Porcuna, 158

Posidonius, 123, 192
pottery, 57, 59, 126, 165–178
  Ampurian grey, 165
  Attic imported, 53, 56
  banded, 59
  'Boquique', 47, 168
  burnished, 47
  channelled, 43
  El Argar type, 165
  geometric, 167–169
  Greek, 58, 99
  impressed, 40, 42, 43
  incised, 45
  Phocaean grey, 165
  South Italian imported, 53
  stab and drag, 168
  wheel turned, 43
Psammeticus I, 181
Pseudo-Scylax, 53
Pseudo-Scymnos, 49, 51
Ptolemy, geographer, 193
Puig de Alcoy, 110
Puig Castellar, plan, 106–107
Punic War, First, 53
Pyrene, 53
Pyrenean culture, 25, 42–43
Pytheas, 17, 191–192
Pythioussas, 52

Redal, 105
Redovan, 58
reguli, 116–117, 118
religion, 16, 40, 59, 131–151
Rhodanussia, 21
Rhode, 17, 52, 127
Rhodes, 51
Rio Tinto mines, 50

Rochina, 26, 99, 110–111
Rojales, sculpture, 158
Roquizal del Rullo, cemetery, 141

Saetabis, 99, 124
Saguntum, 17, 34, 99, 111, 121, 124,
  senate, 118–119
Saint Blaise, 97, 104
Sallust, 65
Salvacañete hoard, 188
San Aleix, 43
San Antonio de Calaceite, 25, 105,
  108
San Cristbal de Mazaleón, 25
  cemetery, 141
San Juliá de Ramis, 99, 101–102
San Miguel de Sorba, 109
sanctuaries, 135–137
Sandars, H., 125
Santiago de la Espada, 133
  hoard, 187–188
Sargon I, King, 49
scarab, 181
Schuchardt, H., 26
Schulten, A., 23–24, 26, 29, 88, 114
Scipio, 62, 74, 117
Sclefilla, 50
sculpture, 126, 152–164
Scylax of Cariadna, 191
Scymnos, 21, 191
Sedetani, 17
Segorbe, 99
Sempronius Gracchus, 62
Sena, 42
Seriña, cave, 42
Sertonius, 62
Setefilla, graves, 45, 46

Sexi, 52
Shalmaneser V, King, 49
sheep, 121
shields, 78–80
shoes, 67
Sicani, 22
Sicily, 54–55
Sidamunt, 137
silos, 109–110
silver,
   brooches, 73
   buckle, 46
   fibula, 46
   mining, 122, 123
   smiths, 127
   vases, 188
Siret, L., 23
Sisapo, 122
solar cults, 131
soliferreum, 80, 81
Spanish Levant, 15, 25, 34, 38, 44–45,
   58–60, 110–111, 118, 143–144
spears, pronged, 83
Sphinx of Haches, 156
sports, 64
spurs, 85
standards, 83–84
stelae, inscribed, 88
Stephanos of Byzantium, 191
Stesichorus, 190
Strabo, 21, 22, 38, 53, 79, 100, 123, 191,
   192
Suessetani, 17, 83, 84, 100
swords, 50, 83, 144
Syracuse, 58

Tanit, statues, 131, 185

Taracena, B., 24
Tarragona, 100, 120, 124
Tarrasa, cemetery, 42
Tarshish, 48, 49, 190.
   See also Tartessos
Tartessians, 16, 25, 35, 47, 50, 89, 115,
   138, 179–186, 191
Tartessos, 17, 29, 34, 48, 51, 114, 116, 122,
   190–192
textile industry, 124
thesauros, 135, 136
Thucydides, 191
Tiberius Gracchus, 62
Tiglath-Pileser, 47
Timaeus, 192
tin trade, 49, 55, 191
Tirsenian, 89
Titi, 34
Tivissa, 110
   jewellery, 188
   phiale, 133–134
   plan of entrance towers, 108
tools, 63
Tovar, A., 27, 87
Toya, graves, 146–150
trade, 126–127
   Andalusian, 59
   metal, 51
   Phoenician, 47–49
   tin, 49–50, 55
trading posts, 56–57
tragula, 80
Tugia, 126
   cemetery, 24, 45, 144
Turdetania, 34, 120, 192
Turdetanians, 35, 62, 66, 75, 115, 117,
   131, 138. *See also* Tartessians

Tutugi, cemetery, 24, 45, 144–146
  amphorae from, 169
  shaft from tomb, 155
Tyre, 47

Ullastret, 28, 53, 54, 97, 99, 102–104
  pottery, 174–175
Urnfields, 41–44, 139–142, 145–146
  culture, 105
Utica, 47

Vasconi, 34
'Vase of the Birds', 172
'Vase of the Dragons', 143, 165
'Vase of the Fish', 143
'Vase of the Goats', 143
'Vase of the Ritual Dance', 170
'Vase of the Startled Horse', 170
'Vase of the two riders', 170
'Vase of the Warriors', 75, 170
vase paintings, 63–70, 77, 169–172
vegetation, 31, 37–39, 121
velites, 81
Velleius Paterculus, 47
Vendrell, cemetery, 140

Verdolay, 75
  belt plaque from, 71–72
  cemetery, 28
  vase painting, 77, 169
  See also El Cabeccio del Tesoro de Ver-
    dolay
Vilallonc de Calaceite, 43
Villaricos, cemetery, 23, 45, 52, 58, 126,
    129, 131, 144–145
vine production, 120
Viriaus, 65, 119, 138
Volsci-Tectosagi, 100
votive offerings, 162–164

wagon wheel, 150
warfare, 73–87
weapons, 16, 41, 77, 80–84
  bronze, 50
weaving, 66, 124
wheel, 150
winged goddesses, 132
writing, 87–96

zoomorphic sculpture, 156–158